BRAIN GAMES™

IMPROVE YOUR MEMORY

Lower Your Brain Age in Minutes a Day

Publications International, Ltd.

Front Cover Photo: Shutterstock
Cover Puzzle: Wayne Robert Williams

Puzzle Constructors: Michael Adams, Cihan Altay, Chris Bolton, Myles Callum, Philip Carter, Gino Collins, Josie Faulkner, The Grabarchuk Family, Luke Haward, Rod Hines, Steve Karp, Kate Mepham, David Millar, Dave Roberts, Marylin Roberts, Stephen Ryder, Gianni Sarcone, Paul Seaburn, Fraser Simpson, Terry Stickels, Jen Torche, Wayne Robert Williams, Alex Willmore

Illustrators: Helem An, Elizabeth Gerber, Robin Humer, Shavan R. Spears, Jen Torche

Introduction: Holli Fort

Louis Weber, CEO
Publications International, Ltd.
7373 North Cicero Avenue
Lincolnwood, Illinois 60712

Permission is never granted for commercial purposes.

ISBN-13: 978-1-4508-1016-6
ISBN-10: 1-4508-1016-0

Manufactured in China.

8 7 6 5 4 3 2 1

Contents

Give your brain a good warm-up with the puzzles in this section.

Boost your brainpower with puzzles that are a little more challenging.

Turn up the heat by doing some heavy mental lifting.

Test the limits of what your mind can do with these demanding brainteasers.

A Cognitive Workout

If you've ever forgotten your car keys—or worse yet, forgotten where you parked your car!—you're not alone. Memory glitches like these happen to everyone, and they can increase as we age and lose memory function. Luckily, memory function can be preserved and even enhanced, and *Brain Games™: Improve Your Memory* can help set you on the right path.

We all know that keeping our bodies in good shape with routine workouts can help us stay young, active, and flexible. It's equally important to put your mind to work in order to keep your brain fit and flexible. Many gerontologists and physicians recommend working puzzles as a great way to do this. In fact, you can think of puzzles as mini workouts for the brain!

Improving your memory is not quite as easy as adding memory to a computer, but then again, your brain is more complicated than even the most sophisticated computer. Scientists have found that exercising the parts of your brain that help retain memories can help you sharpen both your short- and long-term memory skills. For example, the hippocampus is a major part of the brain responsible for forming and storing new memories, whether they're going to be retained for the short term or the long run. There are also two temporal lobes—the right helps preserve visual memory, such as pictures or faces, while the left is responsible for verbal memory, including names and your favorite movie quotations. Keeping these and other parts of your brain fluid and flexible through consistent use is vital for retaining and even improving your memory. And it's hard to think of a more fun and engaging way to get that mental workout than by doing puzzles.

One of the great benefits of using puzzles to improve your memory is that there is such a wide variety to choose from, all of which help energize the memory centers of your brain. The abundance of different puzzles is important because they engage different parts of the brain and combine for an effective overall mental workout. Take a look at just a few of the great puzzles you'll find in this book:

- Number Cross
- Two-Part Recall
- Analogies
- Chain Grid Fill
- Sequencing
- Visual Puzzles
- Word Jigsaws

These puzzles use words, numbers, and visuals to help you flex your "memory muscles," and there are ways for you to further enhance the benefits—and help you solve the puzzles at the same time. For example, scent is a powerful memory trigger, so try associating a word or image with a particular scent to help you remember it. Another twist on this process is to visualize a particular image to go along with a piece of information you don't want to forget. And in the case of trying to remember long numbers, take a tip from the telephone company and try breaking them up into smaller bits. (There's a good reason phone numbers are only seven digits long!)

Keep in mind that the puzzles get more challenging with each level you tackle, offering greater mental benefits. You can further push yourself by working the puzzles at different times of the day, in a variety of locations that have different levels of activity—you might find that it increases the challenge to work a memory puzzle while riding a bus, for example, because of the increased ambient activity. Most importantly, you'll have fun doing something that's not only great for you but may also become an invaluable memory booster.

Stretch Your Mental Muscle

Party Time

ATTENTION | VISUAL SEARCH

There are 10 differences between these party pictures. Can you spot them all?

Answers on page 171.

Number Cross

Use each of the numbers listed here to complete this clue-less crossword grid. The puzzle has only one solution.

3 FIGURES

~~144~~

~~159~~

~~247~~

~~273~~

~~300~~

~~401~~

~~459~~

~~471~~

4 FIGURES

~~1224~~

~~1384~~

~~1613~~

~~2173~~

~~2832~~

~~3067~~

~~3831~~

~~4590~~

5 FIGURES

~~13895~~

~~15363~~

~~15583~~

~~16351~~

~~17256~~

~~23434~~

~~26848~~

~~33310~~

~~35721~~

~~36721~~

~~38798~~

~~42393~~

~~42462~~

~~44269~~

~~45571~~

~~49411~~

6 FIGURES

~~122065~~

~~170631~~

~~172327~~

~~207031~~

~~232674~~

~~233277~~

~~309760~~

~~319213~~

~~334736~~

~~343011~~

~~427152~~

~~441483~~

~~472113~~

~~484985~~

~~498499~~

The completed grid (as filled in by hand):

4	5	1	7	2	2	■	4	4	1 4	8	3
7	■	7	■	1	3	8	9	5	■	8	1
2	3	2	6	7	4	■	4	9	8	4	9
1	■	3	■	3	3	3	1	0	■	9	2
1	2	2	4	■	4	0	1	■	3	8	3
3	6	7	2	1	■	0	■	6	5	5	8
■	8	■	4	5	8	■	2	4	7	■	7
4	4	2	6	9	■	2	■	4	2	3	3
2	8	3	2	■	4	7	1	■	1	3	4
7	■	3	■	1	5	3	6	3	■	4	3
1	2	2	0	6	5	■	3	0	9	7	6
5	■	7	■	1	7	2	5	6	■	3	1
2	0	7	0	3	1	■	1	7	0	6	3

Answer on page 171.

7

Word Jigsaw

Fit the pieces into the frame to form common words reading across and down. There's no need to rotate the pieces; they'll fit as shown, with each piece used once.

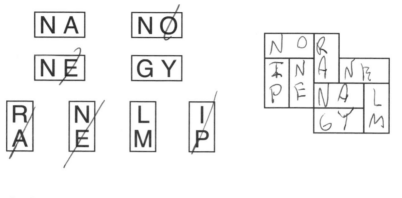

Add-a-Word

Add one word to each of the 3-word sets to create new words or phrases. For example: In a set including "smith," "fore," and "game," the added word would be "word" (creating "wordsmith," "foreword," and "word game").

1. club, jerk, pop: _____

2. fall, tap, bed: _____

3. root, mug, draft: _Myroot Mugdraft_

4. bag, pot, green: _____

5. port, cellar, glass: _glassport_

6. maid, shake, butter: _____

Answers on page 171.

Take a Load Off! (Part 1)

Study these chairs for a minute, then turn the page for a memory challenge.

Armchair

Director's chair

Office chair

Adirondack chair

Folding chair

Stool

Rocking chair

High chair

Take a Load Off! (Part II)   MEMORY

(Do not read this until you have read the previous page!)

Check off the types of chairs you saw on page 9.

___ Barber chair

✓ Couch

✓ Stool

✓ Folding chair

___ Wheelchair

___ Armchair

✓ Rocking chair

___ Office chair

✓ Director's chair

___ Love seat

___ Wicker chair

Number Sequence   ANALYSIS   CREATIVE THINKING

What number completes this sequence?

342 504 126 117 810 135 225 ___

        A. 912

        B. 713

        C. 441

        D. 461

        E. 999

Answers on page 171.

Monsters

Use deductive logic to figure out which monster is which, then determine which one scares each child.

Harry
Monsters with fangs scare me.

Tom
Bogy and Blobby are slimey.

Jane
The big eyes of Blobby scare me.

Kim
I'm afraid of monsters with horns.

Hocus and Blobby have no horns.

I don't like scaring girls.

Stinker and Hocus have fangs.

I scare those with spotty tops.

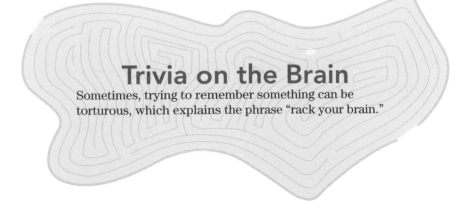

Trivia on the Brain
Sometimes, trying to remember something can be torturous, which explains the phrase "rack your brain."

Cube Fold

CREATIVE THINKING

SPATIAL VISUALIZATION | VISUAL LOGIC

Below is an unfolded cube. Only 2 of the cubes below (marked A–E) can possibly represent this cube when folded. Which 2?

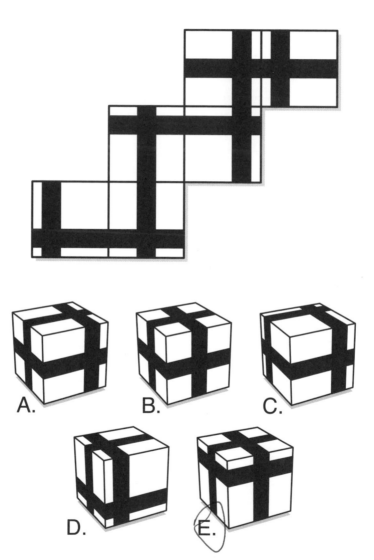

A.

B.

C.

D.

E.

Answers on page 171.

Grid Fill

LANGUAGE / PLANNING

To complete this puzzle, place the given letters and words into the shapes in this grid. Words and letters will run across, down, and wrap around each shape. When the grid is filled, each row will contain one of the following words: braun, dream, fists, patio, sonic, strip.

F	I	S	t	S
B	R	a	v	n
D	C	E	A	M
S	O	N	i	C
P	a	t	I	O
S	t	r	i	P

1. E, I, R, T
2. DR, RI, SA
3. COP, FIB, SON
4. PATS
5. TSUNAMI

Addagram

LANGUAGE

This puzzle functions exactly like an anagram (a word that is a rearrangement of another word) with an added step: In addition to being scrambled, each phrase below is missing the same letter. Discover the missing letter, then unscramble the letters. When you do, you'll reveal the names of 4 cocktails.

I _ _ _ _ _ I   IN TRIM

TARA GRIM

BOY MY LORD

_ _ _ _ _ _ _ _ _ _ _   LIQUEURS SET IN

Number Sequence

ANALYSIS

CREATIVE THINKING

What is the next number in each of the sequences below?

1. 0, 2, 5, 9, 14, ___

  A. 20

  B. 18

  C. 16

2. 2, 4, 8, 10, 14, ___

  A. 18

  B. 20

  C. 16

3. 1, 4, 8, 13, 19, ___

  A. 22

  B. 24

  C. 26

4. 2, 6, 4, 8, 6, ___

  A. 12

  B. 4

  C. 10

Answers on page 171.

Visual Sequence

Which of the lettered figures continues the sequence below?

A.   B.   C.   D.   E.   F.

Pyramid   ANALYSIS   COMPUTATION

The number in each brick is determined by its relationship to the numbers in the row beneath it. Determine what the relationship is and fill in the blank bricks.

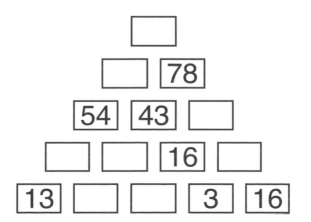

Answers on pages 171–172.

Odd One Out

CREATIVE THINKING

SPATIAL VISUALIZATION · VISUAL LOGIC

Which figure does not belong with the others based on a straight-forward design reason?

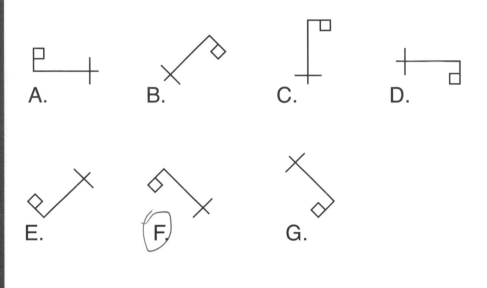

A.   B.   C.   D.

E.   F.   G.

Addagram

LANGUAGE

This puzzle functions exactly like an anagram (a word that is a rearrangement of another word) with an added step: In addition to being scrambled, each word below is missing the same letter. Discover the missing letter, then unscramble the letters. When you do, you'll reveal a lizard, a small particle, a very light dessert, and a racing dog.

AGAIN

ANGLER

REGIMEN

HYDROGEN

Answers on page 172.

Convention of Action Figures (Part I)

MEMORY

Read the following text—paying close attention—before turning the page for a memory challenge.

More than 100 Action Figures showed up at the third annual convention, which of course was held in downtown Jumping Jacks, Wyoming. The Action Figures all had clever comments (or at least terrible pickup lines) for the pretty models who were walking around.

"I'm flipping for you!" said Andy the Acrobat.

"I'm head over wheels for you!" said Rick the Roller Skater.

"I get a kick out of you!" said Max the Martial Artist.

"You're beautiful, and that's no bull!" said Roy the Rodeo Cowboy.

"You got me all pumped up!" said Willie the Weight Lifter.

"Cupid just put an arrow through my heart!" said Arnie the Archer.

"You make me feel so much batter!" said Bob the Baseball Player.

Trivia on the Brain

A long-term study found that people who eat seafood at least once a week have a 30 percent lower risk of developing dementia than their fish-free counterparts.

Convention of Action Figures (Part II)

`MEMORY`

(Do not read this until you have read the previous page!)

Based on the information you read on page 17, answer the following questions:

1. Can you name 3 of the Action Figures' activities (without their first names)?

   <u>ARCHER</u>, <u>weight lifter, Acrobat</u>

2. In what state did the convention take place?

   Jumping Jacks

3. How many annual conventions were held before this one?

   3

Grid Fill

`LANGUAGE` `PLANNING`

To complete this puzzle, place the given letters and words into the shapes in this grid. Words and letters will run across, down, and wrap around each shape. When the grid is filled, each row will contain one of the following words: angry, boast, cigar, stork, table, trees.

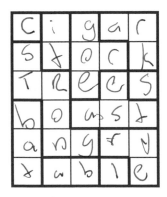

1. C, L, S

2. AB, IT

3. ARK, BAT, RYE

4. EAST, GORE

5. STRONG

Answers on page 172.

Add-a-Word

Add one word to each of the 3-word sets to create new words or
phrases. For example: In a set including "smith," "fore," and "game,"
the added word would be "word" (creating "wordsmith," "foreword,"
and "word game").

1. club, worm, cook: wormclub

2. sob, love, line: sobline

3. folk, teller, tall: tellfolks

4. boy, fair, down: fairboy

5. chain, love, opener: lovechain

6. pad, whole, foot: footpad

Word Jigsaw

Fit the pieces into the frame to form common words reading across
and down. There's no need to rotate the pieces; they'll fit as shown,
with each piece used once.

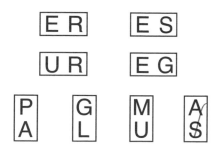

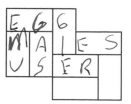

Collection of Cs

ATTENTION | VISUAL SEARCH

Within this picture is a collection of things beginning with the letter **C**. We count 14. How many can you find?

Answers on page 172.

Analogies

Study the relationships of the word pairs to discover what's missing.

1. Fat is to thin as tall is to _chort_
   A. lofty
   B. short
   C. grown

2. Walk is to run as sip is to _drink_
   A. taste
   B. water
   C. drink

3. School is to lesson as theater is to _play_.
   A. play
   B. stage
   C. Broadway

4. Start is to finish as attempt is to _suceed_
   A. try
   B. succeed
   C. begin

Number Sequence

What number is missing from this sequence?

2 1 3 4 _6_

Number Cross

ANALYSIS PLANNING

L
E
V
E
L

1

Use each of the numbers listed here to complete this clue-less crossword grid. The puzzle has only one solution.

3 FIGURES

125

128

154

161

169

219

312

450

4 FIGURES

1371

2964

3010

3113

4043

4300

4848

4853

5 FIGURES

11164

12508

12581

14299

19250

20118

23474

31773

34074

34559

38118

41934

44711

45269

47153

47275

6 FIGURES

130815

139158

146670

150777

216702

241531

246293

268174

303000

390309

428454

430880

431407

474233

483170

Answer on page 172.

Pattern Placement

When meshed together, which 3 patterns below (marked A–F) can form the grid shown in the center? Patterns cannot be rotated or flipped.

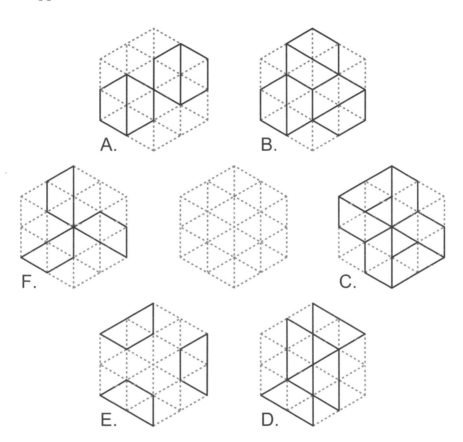

A.

B.

F.

C.

E.

D.

Teddy Bears

ANALYSIS · LOGIC

Use deductive logic to figure out which teddy bear is which, then determine which one belongs to each child.

Alex — Hastings and Alice have patches.

Rory — My Hastings wears a bib.

Laura — My Denis has lost an eye.

June — Martin and Hastings have both eyes.

My human wears a dark top.

My human has curly hair.

My human has a light top.

My human is a girl.

Answer on page 173.

Grid Fill

To complete this puzzle, place the given letters and words into the shapes in this grid. Words and letters will run across, down, and wrap around each shape. When the grid is filled, each row will contain one of the following words: acorn, drone, salad, skate, storm, ultra.

1. D

2. RA, SD

3. MEN, TEA

4. ORAL, ROCK, TORN

5. ASSAULT

Dissection

Separate the figure into 2 identical parts following the grid lines. The parts may be rotated and/or mirrored.

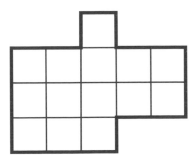

LEVEL 1

L
E
V
E
L

1

What to Wear?

This lady is getting ready to go out for the evening and can't decide which shoes to wear. She has lots of the same pair but which does she own the most of?

Answer on page 173.

Mind Stretcher

Which choice belongs in the last circle?

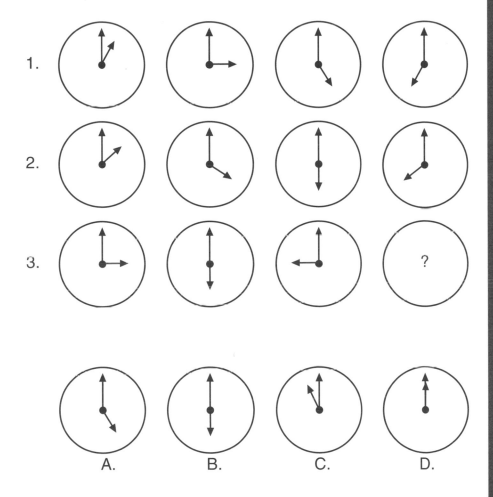

Analogies

CREATIVE THINKING   GENERAL KNOWLEDGE

Study the relationships of the word pairs to discover what's missing.

1. Meeting is to agenda as trip is to _____.
    A. journey
    B. fall
    C. map

2. Sniff is to smell as _____ is to taste.
    A. lick
    B. tongue
    C. nose

3. Tired is to sleep as _____ is to eat.
    A. food
    B. hungry
    C. flavor

4. Pen is to write as knife is to _____.
    A. fork
    B. sharp
    C. cut

Trivia on the Brain

Oxford University researchers have suggested that after a trauma there's a 6-hour window when memory formation can be disrupted. Subjects played the video game *Tetris* to use up some of the cognitive power that their brains would normally be using to create memories.

Answers on page 173.

Game Board (Part I)

Study this game board for one minute, particularly the shapes and their placement. Then turn the page for a memory challenge.

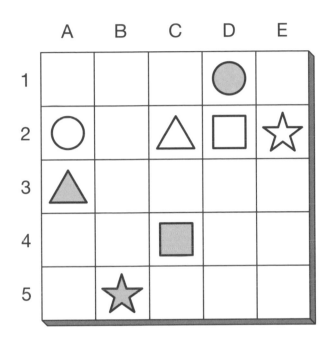

Game Board (Part II)

MEMORY

(Do not read this until you have read the previous page!)

Duplicate the board as seen on page 29.

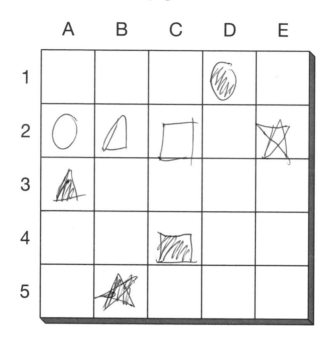

Max-Die-Sum

ANALYSIS LOGIC

What is the maximum sum of a common die's pips that can be seen simultaneously? No mirror or special tricks can be used.

Answers on page 173.

Number Cross

ANALYSIS PLANNING

Use each of the numbers listed here to complete this clue-less crossword grid. The puzzle has only one solution.

3 FIGURES

130

192

355

386

394

489

534

553

4 FIGURES

1170

1809

2072

2455

4134

4354

5223

5824

5 FIGURES

13031

18364

18454

18671

23462

26514

29032

36134

37359

38888

42159

46350

48525

53017

56565

56992

6 FIGURES

117221

117332

152733

187525

238029

315385

359540

379938

408877

425528

449058

495241

509550

582555

588051

Answer on page 173.

Broken Heart

ANALYSIS   LOGIC

Is it possible to divide the heart into 2 identical shapes by separating it only along the white grid lines?

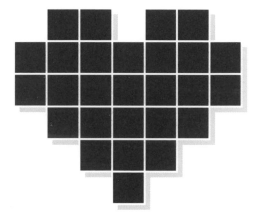

Mystery List

ANALYSIS   LOGIC

Larry just received an e-mail from his nephew Billy with the following wish list of presents for his sixth birthday.

fph

nolr

dlsyrnpstf

ypu tpnpy

o[pf

Clearly, something is wrong with this list. Can you help Larry determine what Billy really wants?

Answers on page 173.

Beastly Metaphors (Part I)

Read the following text—paying close attention—before turning the page for a memory challenge.

You may be busy as a bee, but we know you're not a birdbrain. So here are some animal metaphors for all you eager beavers.

Ever hear of a Judas goat? As the name implies, it's a kind of traitor, a goat that's trained to herd other animals (such as sheep or cattle) to a specific destination, sometimes even a slaughterhouse.

We hope you've never cried crocodile tears. They indicate a false or insincere display of emotion, such as a hypocrite crying fake tears of grief.

Should you bet on a dark horse? Maybe. It just means a horse or a political candidate about which little is known. Many a dark horse has emerged to sudden prominence. (Abraham Lincoln was actually a dark-horse candidate when he ran for president.)

Have you ever "put on the dog"? It means to dress up, get all fancy, or make a flashy display. If you put on the dog, will you be the cat's meow or the bee's knees? Either way, you'll be happy as a clam!

Beastly Metaphors (Part II)

MEMORY

(Do not read this until you have read the previous page!)

Based on the information you read on page 33, answer the following questions:

1. Crocodile tears are (A) a large flying insect (B) a false display of emotion (C) a liquid detergent (D) a cocktail.

2. A dark horse is (A) Black Beauty (B) Man o' War (C) John F. Kennedy (D) a little-known person or thing.

3. A Judas goat is (A) a biblical beast (B) Iscariot's favorite pet (C) a goat trained to herd other animals (D) a type of cheese.

4. "Putting on the dog" means (A) wearing a canine costume (B) looking like the Big Bad Wolf (C) putting on a fancy display (D) kidding Fido.

Number Sequence

ANALYSIS

CREATIVE THINKING

What number comes next?

10 17 26 37 50 65 ___

A. 72

B. 73

C. 80

D. 82

Answers on pages 173–174.

Add-a-Word

ANALYSIS   LANGUAGE

Add one word to each of the 3-word sets to create new words or phrases. For example: In a set including "smith," "fore," and "game," the added word would be "word" (creating "wordsmith," "foreword," and "word game").

1. lame, tail, cold: _duck_

2. bumps, step, mother: _goose_

3. dive, song, black: _swan_

4. turtle, tail, cote: _dove_

5. hole, clay, stool: _pigeon_

6. double, spread, scout: _eagle_

Word Jigsaw

LANGUAGE   PLANNING

Fit the pieces into the frame to form common words reading across and down. There's no need to rotate the pieces; they'll fit as shown, with each piece used once.

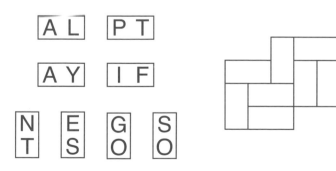

L
E
V
E
L

1

Cube Count

CREATIVE THINKING

SPATIAL VISUALIZATION   VISUAL LOGIC

How many individual cubes are in the stack below? Assume all rows and columns run to completion unless you see them end.

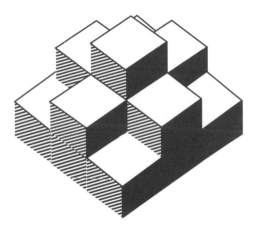

It's a Big Block

CREATIVE THINKING   LOGIC

My house is ninth from one end of the row and third from the other end. How many houses are there in the row?

Answers on page 174.

Analogies

Study the relationships of the word pairs to discover what's missing.

1. Trade is to barter as build is to _____.
   A. construct
   B. demolish
   C. sell

2. Express is to say as believe is to _____.
   A. doubt
   B. truth
   C. think

3. Chase is to catch as _____ is to find.
   A. search
   B. discover
   C. lose

4. Mumble is to speak as hum is to _____.
   A. music
   B. sing
   C. snore

Trivia on the Brain

Prolonged stress can kill cells in the hippocampus, the part of the brain that's critical for memory. Thankfully, we're able to grow new neurons in this area again, even as adults.

Answers on page 174.

LEVEL 1

Quilt Quest

CREATIVE THINKING

SPATIAL VISUALIZATION · VISUAL LOGIC

The small, tricolored shape on the bottom appears 3 times in the quilt below. Find all 3 instances. The shape can be rotated but not mirrored.

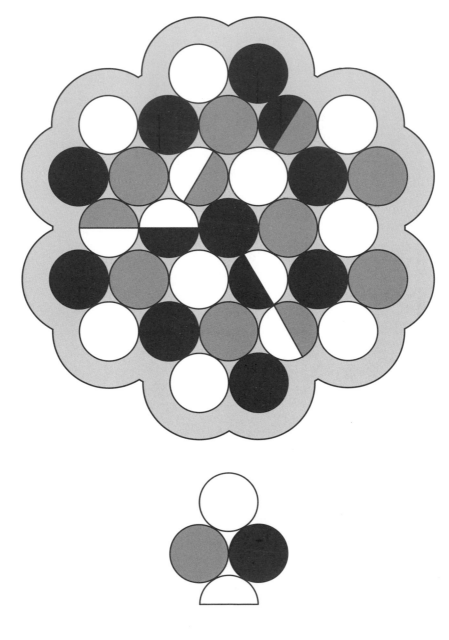

Answer on page 174.

Odd One Out

CREATIVE THINKING
SPATIAL VISUALIZATION   VISUAL LOGIC

Which is the odd one out?

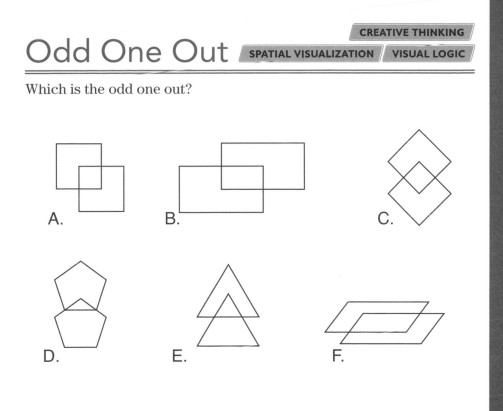

A.

B.

C.

D.

E.

F.

After the Rain

CREATIVE THINKING   LOGIC

At 8:00 P.M., it's raining in New York City. What are the chances of seeing a colorful rainbow 5 hours later?

Too Dark

Fitting Words

L
E
V
E
L

1

In this miniature crossword, the clues are listed randomly and are numbered for convenience only. It is up to you to figure out the placement of the 9 answers. To help you, we've inserted one letter in the grid, and this is the only occurrence of that letter in the completed puzzle.

CLUES

1. Domesticates
2. Off-limits
3. Seep
4. Take by force
5. Region
6. Bauxite and others
7. Baseball boo-boo
8. Fedora feature
9. Kind of pilot

Trivia on the Brain

Back in medieval times, to make sure significant events weren't forgotten, adults would show a young child important procedures very carefully and then throw them into a river. Supposedly, the traumatic experience would ensure that the memory would not be forgotten for as long as the child lived. We don't suggest you try this at home!

Answer on page 174.

Quipu

Which of the 3 Quipus (Incan devices for recording information) is identical to the one in the frame? Quipus are considered identical when they can be matched perfectly only by rotating pieces around the knots—they cannot be lifted or turned over. See the examples for further clarification.

EXAMPLE 1

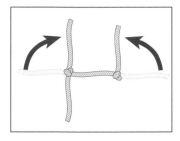

EXAMPLE 2

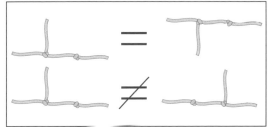

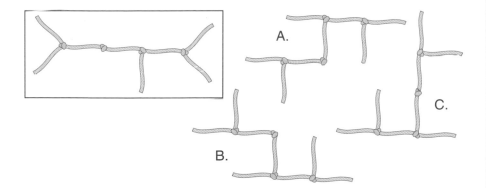

A.

C.

B.

Answer on page 174.

Word Jigsaw

LANGUAGE   PLANNING

Fit the pieces into the frame to form common words reading across and down. There's no need to rotate the pieces; they'll fit as shown, with each piece used once.

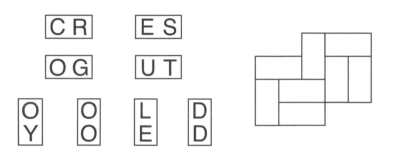

Deal Me In

ANALYSIS   CREATIVE THINKING

Can you complete the sequence below?

C, D, H, ___

Answers on page 174.

Moon Base (Part I)

Study the lunar schematics and their names before turning the page for a memory challenge.

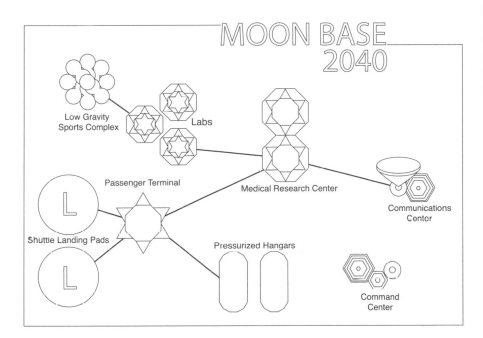

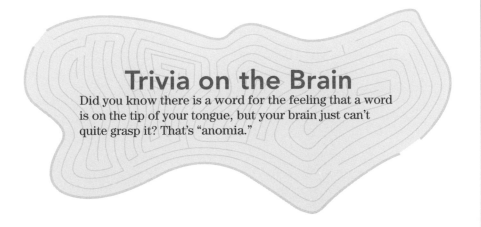

Trivia on the Brain

Did you know there is a word for the feeling that a word is on the tip of your tongue, but your brain just can't quite grasp it? That's "anomia."

L
E
V
E
L

1

Moon Base (Part II)

(Do not read this until you have read the previous page!)

Now that you've studied the schematics, fill in the names of the buildings as they were labeled on the previous page.

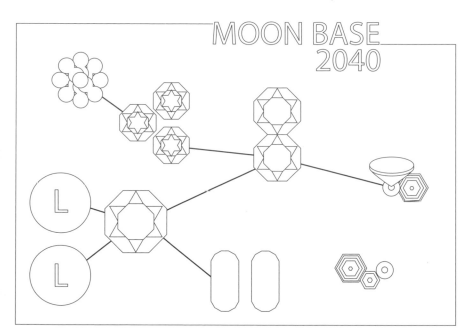

Squared Cubes Squared

ANALYSIS   COMPUTATION

Which is larger, a dozen dozen squared then cubed, or a dozen dozen cubed then squared? Or are they equal?

Answers on page 174.

What Comes Next?

Which figure completes this sequence?

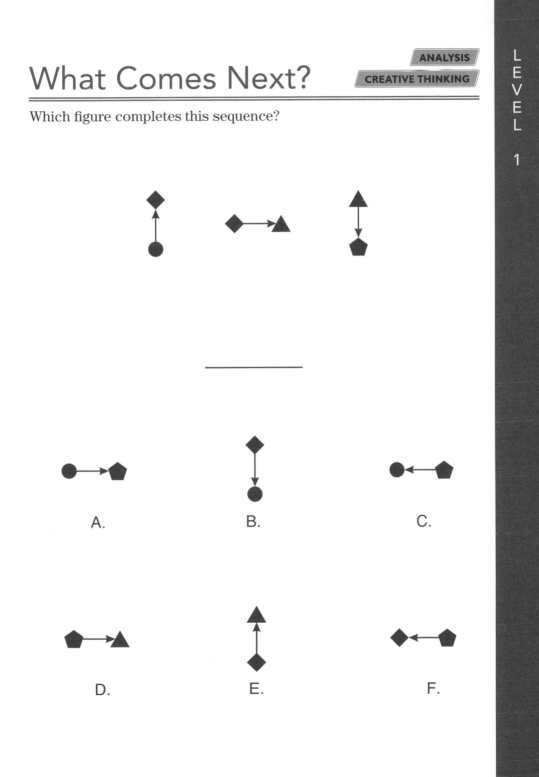

A.

B.

C.

D.

E.

F.

Get Your Memory Moving
Letter Logic

ANALYSIS PLANNING

Use each of the words, names, and acronyms listed here to complete this clue-less crossword grid. The puzzle has only one solution.

3 LETTERS
CAT
EYE
OAT
SEE

4 LETTERS
BAIT
BARK
BEAD
BOSS
CASK
DARK
GLUE
GREY
MOAT
ODIN
PACE
PEAR
TASK
ZEUS

5 LETTERS
ACORN
AISLE
ALBUM
AMBER
BLESS
BLUES
CHARM
CHIME
CREPE

DRAMA
ELECT
EXAMS
EXTRA
INDIA
LASSO

MOUTH
OFTEN
RHYME
SITAR
SPITZ
STOVE

TABOO
TONIC
TREAT
UNITY
WHOLE
WORLD

Answer on page 175.

6 LETTERS
BRAZIL
CLICHÉ
EDITOR
GARGLE
PLOUGH
PREFER
RECIPE
SEXTET

7 LETTERS
ANCHOVY
APRICOT
COLLAGE
CONFESS
EXPENSE
OVATION
PREMIER

ROULADE
SEAGULL
SHELTER
STILTON
TORONTO
TRACTOR
TRIBUTE

8 LETTERS
CONSOMMÉ
DISPATCH
ESCARGOT
REGIONAL

9 LETTERS
NOSTALGIA

Sleepless in Seattle

This poor guy can't sleep with all the things wrong in his room!
Can you find all 10?

L
E
V
E
L

2

Missing Number ANALYSIS COMPUTATION

Based on an established pattern, what number should replace the question mark in the last figure?

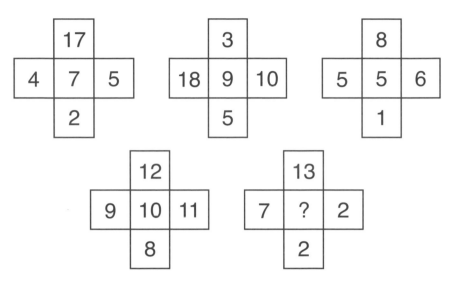

Dissection CREATIVE THINKING SPATIAL VISUALIZATION VISUAL LOGIC

Separate the figure into 5 identical parts following the grid lines. The parts may be rotated and/or mirrored.

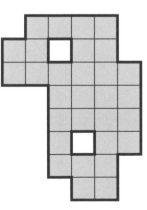

Answers on page 175.

How Many?

How many triangles of any size can you count in the figure below?

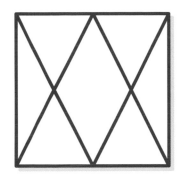

Grid Fill

To complete this puzzle, place the given letters and words into the shapes in this grid. Words and letters will run across, down, and wrap around each shape. When the grid is filled, each row will contain one of the following words: beast, choir, crams, drape, happy, icing.

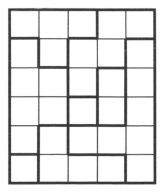

1. D, O

2. PI

3. BEAR, CRAP

4. STAMP

5. CHACHI

6. SYRINGE

L
E
V
E
L

2

Visual Sequence ANALYSIS CREATIVE THINKING

Which of the lettered figures continues the sequence?

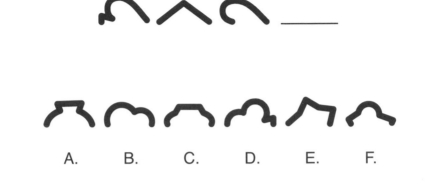

A.   B.   C.   D.   E.   F.

Fitting Words GENERAL KNOWLEDGE PLANNING

In this miniature crossword, the clues are listed randomly and are numbered for convenience only. It is up to you to figure out the placement of the 9 answers. To help you, we've inserted one letter in the grid, and this is the only occurrence of that letter in the completed puzzle.

CLUES

1. Baby-bringing bird
2. ____ and kicking
3. At any time
4. Short snoozes
5. Metric prefix meaning 1,000
6. Heaps
7. Office furniture
8. Came to the ground
9. In the buff

Answers on page 175.

Number Cross

Use each of the numbers listed here to complete this clue-less crossword grid. The puzzle has only one solution.

3 FIGURES

130

192

230

249

293

343

401

503

4 FIGURES

1017

1485

2442

3415

3748

4160

5908

5926

5 FIGURES

20484

22530

28128

31738

31985

38433

39322

40524

40851

41211

41220

43330

45531

50291

51227

52320

6 FIGURES

151294

259184

312010

319745

341978

350264

383874

415924

442103

498941

516555

560688

561110

579912

590777

Answer on page 176.

Cube Fold

CREATIVE THINKING

SPATIAL VISUALIZATION   VISUAL LOGIC

Below is an unfolded cube. Only 2 of the cubes below (marked A–E) can possibly represent this cube when folded. Which 2?

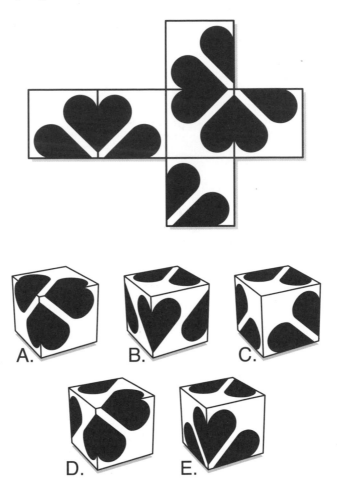

A.

B.

C.

D.

E.

Answers on page 176.

Area Code

Which has a larger area, a circle with a radius of 2 or a circle with a diameter of 4?

Hearty Greetings (Part I)

This heart-shaped crossword is filled with terms of endearment. Study it for a minute, then turn the page for a memory challenge.

Answer on page 176.

Hearty Greetings (Part II)   MEMORY

(Do not read this until you have read the previous page!)

Check off the words you saw on page 53.

___ Chick

___ Honeybun

✓ Love

✓ Sweetheart

___ Roses

✓ Chocolate

___ Honey

___ Baby doll

___ Sweetie

___ Valentine card

___ Lamb

___ Precious

___ Pet

Word Jigsaw   LANGUAGE   PLANNING

Fit the pieces into the frame to form common words reading across and down. There's no need to rotate the pieces; they'll fit as shown, with each piece used once.

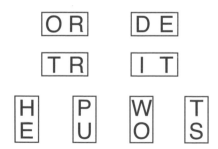

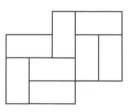

Answers on page 176.

Curve Fill

Fill in each heavy-outlined set of cells with the same number (0, 2, or 5) so that the sums given for each curved row and column and the 2 sections extending from the center oval are true. For further insight, see the example puzzle.

EXAMPLE

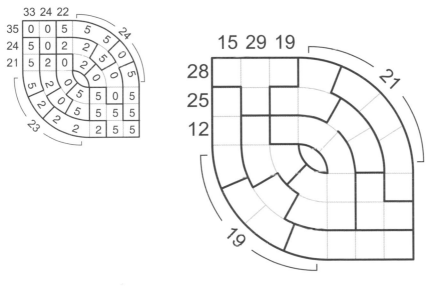

Add-a-Word

Add one word to each of the 3-word sets to create new words or phrases. For example: In a set including "smith," "fore," and "game," the added word would be "word" (creating "wordsmith," "foreword," and "word game").

1. grand, bar, player: _____

2. major, ear, hum: _____

3. shoe, pipe, bull: _____

4. stop, wolf, penny: _____

5. machine, metal, squirt: _____

Answers on page 176.

Cat Finder

LEVEL 2

Use deductive logic to figure out which cat is which, then determine which one belongs to each person.

Penny
My Kitty has dark fur.

Poppy
I just bought my cat a new collar.

Paul
Lila and Tiffany wear collars.

Peter
My Felix is always playing with toy mice.

My owner always wears glasses.

My owner wears spots.

I'd never have an owner who wore spots.

Felix and Lila are snow white.

Number Sequence

What number is missing from this sequence?

15 9 6 3 ___

Answers on page 176.

Dot Movement

If the black ball in the figure below moves clockwise one vertex on each move, and the white ball moves 2 vertices counterclockwise on each move, where will each be after 5 moves?

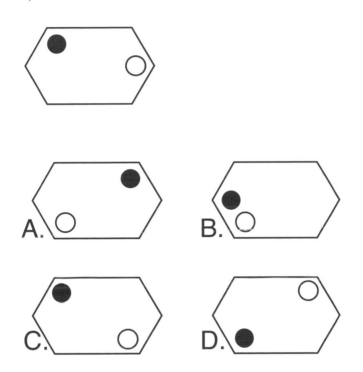

Trivia on the Brain

Napping isn't just for kids! Recent studies show that adults who indulged in midday naps performed 20 percent better on memory exercises than those who did not nap.

Answer on page 176.

Analogies

CREATIVE THINKING **GENERAL KNOWLEDGE**

Study the relationships of the word pairs to discover what's missing.

1. Desert is to dry as water is to _____.
   - A. flow
   - B. wet
   - C. cooler

2. Saw is to cut as hammer is to _____.
   - A. pound
   - B. metal
   - C. nail

3. Yawn is to boredom as smile is to _____.
   - A. lips
   - B. grin
   - C. amusement

4. Mongrel is to poodle as alloy is to _____.
   - A. steel
   - B. iron
   - C. mutt

Cast-a-Word

LOGIC **PROBLEM SOLVING**

There are 4 dice, and there are different letters of the alphabet on the 6 faces of each of them (each letter appears only once). Random throws of the dice produced the words in this list. Can you figure out which letters appear on each of the 4 dice?

BONE	DIRE	MAXI	SHAM
BREW	GOLF	POXY	TONG
CLAM	KNOB	PROF	VASE
CURD	LOBE	QUIT	WEAN

Answers on page 176.

Pattern Placement

CREATIVE THINKING
SPATIAL VISUALIZATION · VISUAL LOGIC

When meshed together, which 3 patterns below (marked A–F) can form the grid shown in the center? Patterns cannot be rotated or flipped.

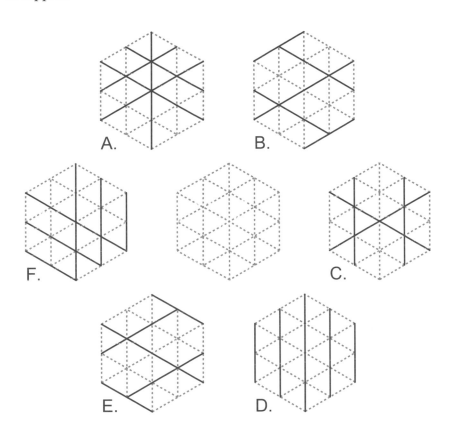

A.

B.

F.

C.

E.

D.

Dart Toss

Using the figure below, if you were to throw a dart at 4 different numbers that add up to 100, one of the numbers that it could not be is:

A. 44   B. 12   C. 18   D. 23

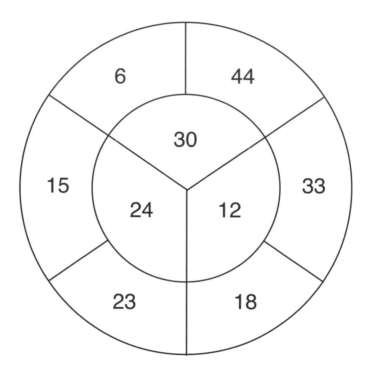

Trivia on the Brain

Common wisdom has long held that goldfish have a memory span of only 3 seconds. Not true: In addition to more scientific research, the television show *Mythbusters* showed that a goldfish could remember the way through an obstacle course for at least a month.

Answer on page 177.

Round Trip (Part I)

Study these items for a minute, then turn the page for a memory challenge. Remember the item pictured, not the caption.

Mermaid

Dictionary

Trumpet

Lizard

Safety pin

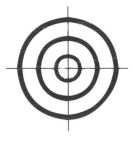

Cell phone

Pencil

Lightbulb

Round Trip (Part II)

MEMORY

(Do not read this until you have read the previous page!)

Check off the items you saw on page 61.

___ Tomato

___ Disco ball

___ Button

___ Gumdrop

___ Computer

___ Globe

___ Target in crosshairs

___ Mermaid

___ Bottle cap

___ Basketball

___ Yin and yang symbol

Fitting Words

GENERAL KNOWLEDGE   PLANNING

In this miniature crossword, the clues are listed randomly and are numbered for convenience only. It is up to you to figure out the placement of the 9 answers. To help you, we've inserted one letter in the grid, and this is the only occurrence of that letter in the completed puzzle.

CLUES

1. Destitute
2. "Do _____ others..."
3. Restaurant reservation
4. Henna user
5. Playful river creature
6. Financial burden
7. Reversed the effects of
8. Run in neutral
9. Tidy

Answers on page 177.

Odd One Out

CREATIVE THINKING · SPATIAL VISUALIZATION · VISUAL LOGIC

One of the following figures doesn't belong with the others, based on a simple design. Which is the odd one out? Hint: This does not have to do with symmetry or the fact that B has no sides.

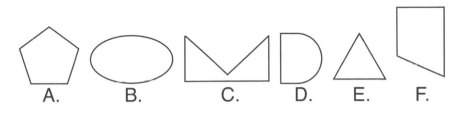

A. B. C. D. E. F.

Quipu

ANALYSIS · LOGIC

Which of the 3 Quipus (Incan devices for recording information) is identical to the one in the frame? Quipus are considered identical when they can be matched perfectly only by rotating pieces around the knots—they cannot be lifted or turned over. See the examples for further clarification.

EXAMPLE 1   **EXAMPLE 2**

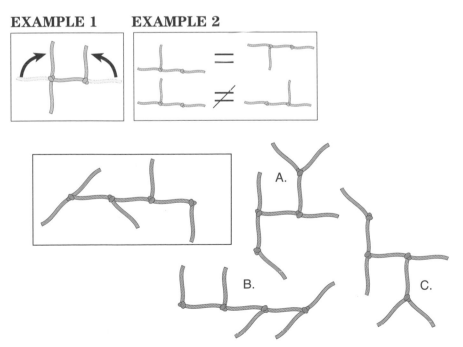

Cube Fold

CREATIVE THINKING

SPATIAL VISUALIZATION | VISUAL LOGIC

Below is an unfolded cube. Only 2 of the cubes below (marked A–E) can possibly represent this cube when folded. Which 2?

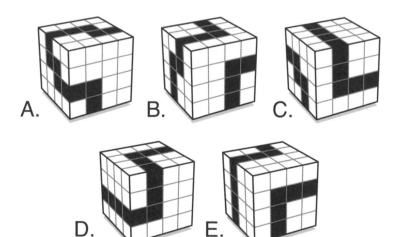

A.

B.

C.

D.

E.

Answer on page 177.

Bottled Up

The sealed 400-milliliter bottle on the left contains 220 milliliters of water. The water level is marked by the dotted line. When the bottle is turned over, will the level rest at mark A, B, or C?

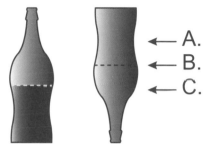

Role Models (Part I)

Read the following text—paying close attention—before turning the page for a memory challenge.

Charlie Chan, the Asian detective created by author Earl Derr Biggers, wasn't entirely fictional. Biggers patterned him after a real-life Honolulu detective named Chang Apana that he read about in a newspaper.

Robinson Crusoe, the title hero of Daniel Defoe's novel, was inspired by Alexander Selkirk (1676–1721), a Scottish sailor. Selkirk signed on with an expedition to the South Seas but quarreled with his captain. In October 1704, at his own request, he was put ashore on Mas-a-Tierra, a small uninhabited island in the Juan Fernandez group. He lived alone on the island until he was picked up more than 4 years later.

Nora Charles, the wife of Nick Charles in Dashiell Hammett's *The Thin Man*, was modeled after Lillian Hellman (1905–1984), the American playwright (*Toys in the Attic*). Hellman was romantically involved with Hammett for 30 years.

Answer on page 177.

Role Models (Part II)

MEMORY

(Do not read this until you have read the previous page!)

Based on the information you read on page 65, answer the following questions:

1. What novel was based on the life of Alexander Selkirk?

2. Chang Apana was a detective in what U.S. city?

3. In what Hammett story do Nick and Nora Charles appear?

4. What detective was created by Earl Derr Biggers?

5. How long did Alexander Selkirk live alone on an island?

Word Jigsaw

LANGUAGE   PLANNING

Fit the pieces into the frame to form common words reading across and down. There's no need to rotate the pieces; they'll fit as shown, with each piece used once.

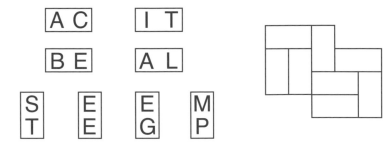

Answers on page 177.

Analogies

Study the relationships of the word pairs to discover what's missing.

1. Pillar is to building as _____ is to table.
   A. chair
   B. leg
   C. furniture

2. Knight is to courageous as hurricane is to _____.
   A. weather
   B. tornado
   C. dangerous

3. Retreat is to advance as _____ is to survive.
   A. perish
   B. kill
   C. flourish

4. Sudden is to gradual as toss is to _____.
   A. throw
   B. sprinkle
   C. quick

Perfect Circle

When joined together without overlapping, will these 2 pieces form a perfect circle?

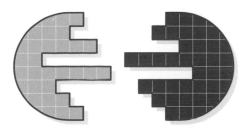

Add-a-Word

ANALYSIS | LANGUAGE

Add one word to each of the 3-word sets to create new words or phrases. For example: In a set including "smith," "fore," and "game," the added word would be "word" (creating "wordsmith," "foreword," and "word game").

1. pile, ant, slave: _____

2. house, fan, health: _____

3. winter, beret, bean: _____

4. door, mouse, clap: _____

5. park, fast, snow: _____

6. lone, pack, timber: _____

Matching Sticks

ANALYSIS | LOGIC

Is it possible from 5 matchsticks to make 10 (without breaking the matchsticks)?

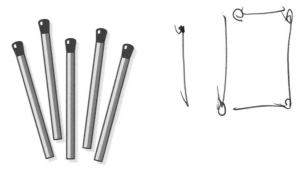

Answers on page 177.

Place Settings

Forty-six people are numbered 1 through 46 and placed around a circular table in numerical order. What is the number of the person directly opposite the person whose number is 13?

A. 21   B. 22   C. 34   D. 36   E. 40

Game Board (Part I)

MEMORY

Study this game board for one minute, particularly the shapes and their placement. Then turn the page for a memory challenge.

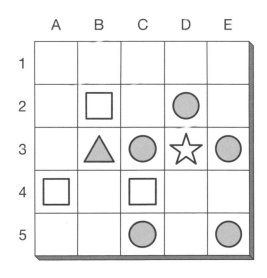

Game Board (Part II)

(Do not read this until you have read the previous page!)

Duplicate the board as seen on page 69.

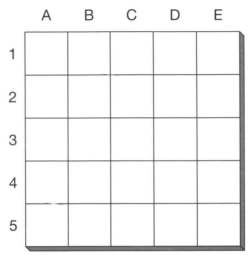

What Comes Next?

ANALYSIS

CREATIVE THINKING

Study the series of letters below. Every letter in each series is the first letter of a word, and all the words in each series are related. For example, if the first 4 letters of a series were M, V, E, M, they could stand for Mercury, Venus, Earth, and Mars. Logically, the next letter would be J, for Jupiter.

Continue each series below by discovering the next logical word.

1. G, E, L, N, D, J, J, ___

2. P, C, F, S, T, S, L, C, ___

3. Y, B, R, P, O, G, B, ___

Answers on page 178.

Square Search

There are 11 different squares of various sizes contained within the dots below. We've given you 9 squares, 5 on the bottom left and 4 on the bottom right. Can you find the other 2?

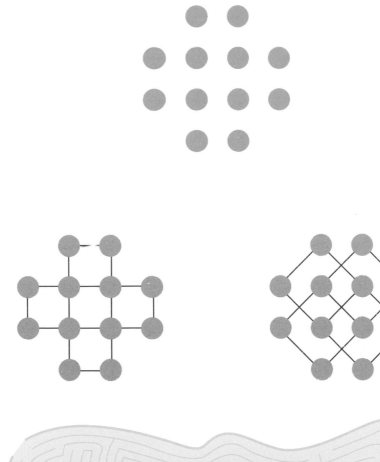

Trivia on the Brain

The stress caused by frequent jet lag and changing work hours (such as that experienced by airline employees and shift workers) can damage memory and the temporal lobe of the brain.

Answer on page 178.

Square Donut   `ANALYSIS` `LOGIC`

The 3-D figure consists of 8 cubes. If you could pick this up and turn it around, how many square outlines of all possible sizes would you be able to recognize on the entire figure?

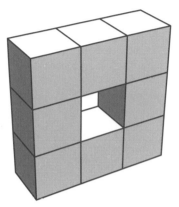

Analogies   `CREATIVE THINKING` `GENERAL KNOWLEDGE`

Study the relationships of the word pairs to discover what's missing.

1. Courtroom is to judge as _____ is to police officer.
   A. badge
   B. precinct
   C. crime

2. Child is to family as student is to _____.
   A. teacher
   B. lesson
   C. class

3. Wheat is to bread as milk is to _____.
   A. cheese
   B. dairy
   C. cow

Answers on page 178.

Pythagorize It!

Blacken one white dot within the board so that from this dot exactly 4 symmetrical squares can be drawn. Squares must be drawn along the black dots. See the example illustration for clarification.

EXAMPLE

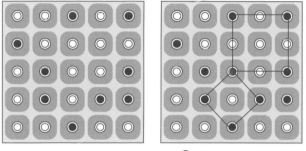

● extra blackened dot

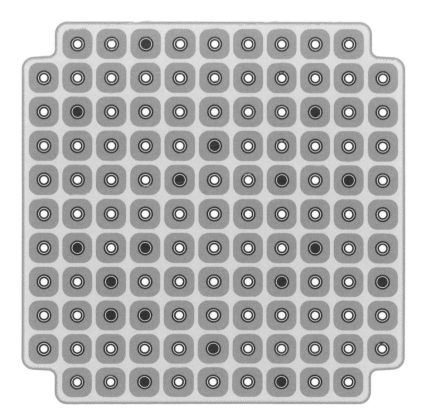

Letter Logic

Use each of the words, names, and acronyms listed here to complete this clue-less crossword grid. The puzzle has only one solution.

LEVEL 2

3 LETTERS
KIT
NAY

4 LETTERS
ARCH
BEST
BLUR
EPIC
FAME
FETE
FROG
HAND
LARK
ROOM
SNAP
ZONE

5 LETTERS
ANKLE
APPLE
BLEND
CHESS
COAST
CUPID
EAGER
EASEL
HOUSE
HYENA
LARCH
PLEAT

RUCHE
SHELL
SHOES
SKATE
SKIRT

SMASH
SMILE
STYLE
THYME
VISOR

6 LETTERS
HOSTEL
REFUND
SESAME
SHERRY

Answer on page 178.

TURTLE
YIELDS

7 LETTERS
DOLLARS
EMBROIL
HARVEST

IMPROVE
LECTERN
LEISURE
NERVOUS
ROMANCE
ROMANIA

SERVANT
SHAMPOO
SKY BLUE
TARNISH
THERAPY

8 LETTERS
BARNACLE
DRUMROLL
DUTY-FREE
EGGSHELL
LIPSTICK
REMEMBER

How Many?

ANALYSIS   COMPUTATION

How many triangles of any size can you count in the figure below?

A. 16   B. 17   C. 25   D. 27   E. 43

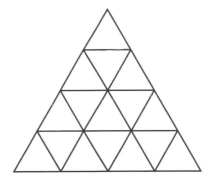

Answer on page 179.

LEVEL 2

Grid Fill

LANGUAGE PLANNING

To complete this puzzle, place the given letters and words into the shapes in this grid. Words and letters will run across, down, and wrap around each shape. When the grid is filled, each row will contain one of the following words: again, berry, blimp, draft, enter, frame.

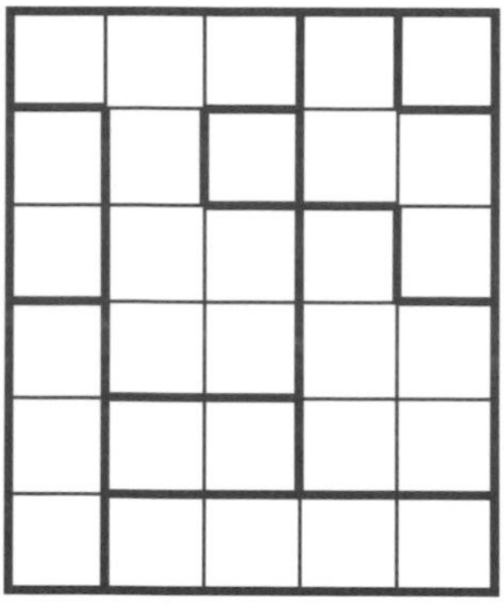

1. A, E
2. AD, ER
3. EBB
4. LIMP, MINT
5. FERRY
6. FRAGRANT

Longest Snake

CREATIVE THINKING

SPATIAL VISUALIZATION VISUAL LOGIC

Which snake is the longest?

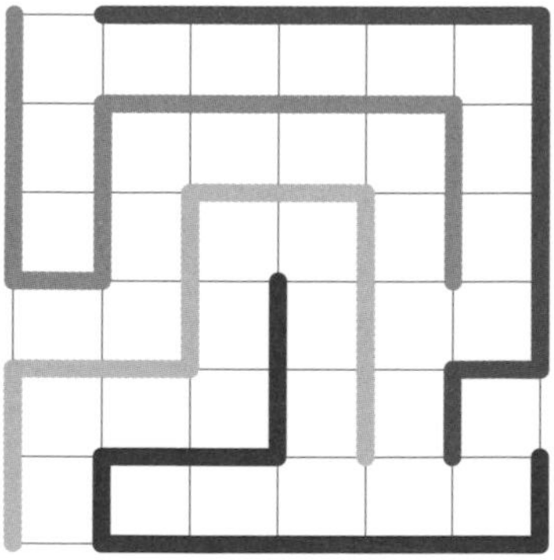

Answers on page 179.

Number Sequence

What is the next number in each of the sequences below?

1. 3, 6, 12, 15, 21, ___
   A. 24
   B. 27
   C. 31

2. 6, 11, 15, 18, 20, ___
   A. 23
   B. 21
   C. 26

3. 1, 3, 7, 13, 21, ___
   A. 31
   B. 24
   C. 26

4. 2, 13, 35, 68, 112, ___
   A. 132
   B. 144
   C. 167

Trivia on the Brain

Talk about a brain game! Former World Memory Champion Ben Pridmore of England took only 5 minutes to memorize the dates of 96 historical events. He also memorized a shuffled deck of playing cards in just 26.28 seconds.

Answers on page 179.

Odd One Out

CREATIVE THINKING · SPATIAL VISUALIZATION · VISUAL LOGIC

Which shape doesn't belong?

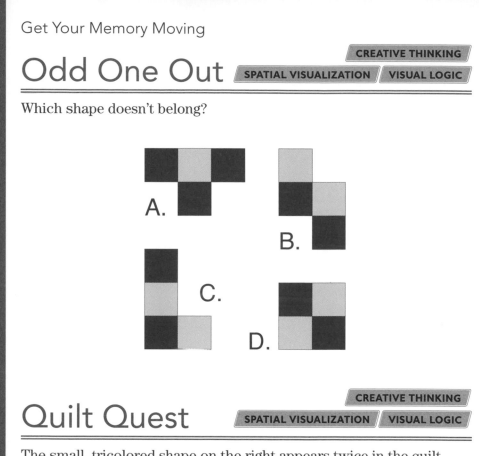

Quilt Quest

CREATIVE THINKING · SPATIAL VISUALIZATION · VISUAL LOGIC

The small, tricolored shape on the right appears twice in the quilt below. Find both instances. The shape can be rotated but not mirrored.

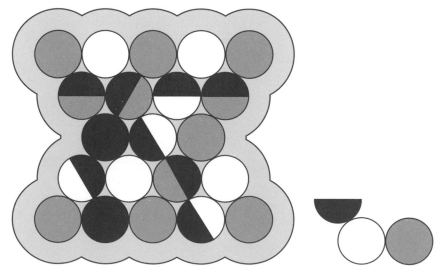

Answers on page 179.

Analogies

Study the relationships of the word pairs to discover what's missing.

1. Petal is to flower as _____ is to tree.
   A. wood
   B. forest
   C. leaf

2. Spark is to wildfire as _____ is to blizzard.
   A. snowflake
   B. weather
   C. wind

3. Master is to servant as sovereign is to _____.
   A. subject
   B. queen
   C. monarch

4. Couch is to furniture as bass is to _____.
   A. gills
   B. trout
   C. fish

Days of the Week

In a random 10-day period, what is the maximum number of times a day can repeat?

A. 1

B. 2

C. 3

Answers on page 179.

Visual Sequence `ANALYSIS` `CREATIVE THINKING`

Which of the lettered figures below continues this sequence?

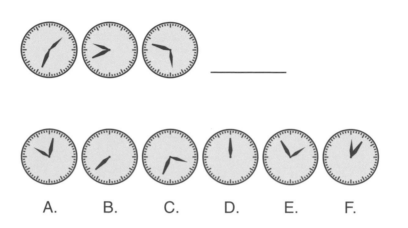

A. B. C. D. E. F.

Marathon `ANALYSIS` `LOGIC`

Alyssa ran a marathon in which she finished both 23rd from the top and 23rd from the bottom. How many people were in the race?

A. 40

B. 45

C. 46

D. 47

E. Impossible to know

Answers on page 179.

Number Cross

ANALYSIS PLANNING

Use each of the numbers listed here to complete this clue-less crossword grid. The puzzle has only one solution.

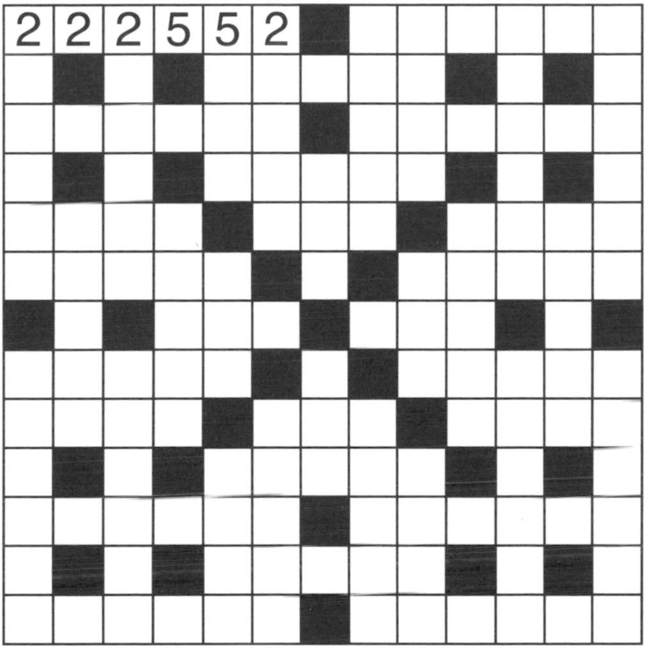

3 FIGURES
179
193
240
241
374
448
491
544

4 FIGURES
1240
1323
2875
2925
3525
3617
3675
5322

5 FIGURES
11271
14302
14501
17802
21187
23254
24747
25170
33712
34042
35199
40483
46141
54395
56856
57619

6 FIGURES
113294
158826
177197
197739
249166
256921
271967
282734
286322
334541
350786
481148
486577
531136
592187

Answer on page 179.

Koi Pond

ATTENTION | VISUAL SEARCH

L
E
V
E
L

2

Some things have changed in these tranquil koi scenes—can you find all 15 differences?

Answers on page 179.

Quipu

Which of the 3 Quipus (Incan devices for recording information) is identical to the one in the frame? Quipus are considered identical when they can be matched perfectly only by rotating pieces around the knots—they cannot be lifted or turned over. See the examples for further clarification.

EXAMPLE 1

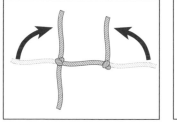

EXAMPLE 2

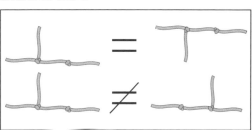

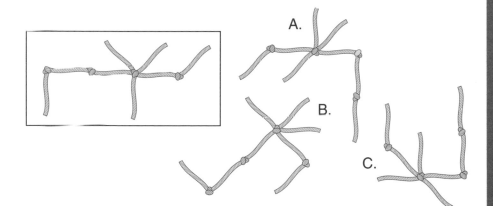

A.

B.

C.

Cube Paint

If 2 gallons of paint are needed to cover all the sides of one cube, how many gallons are needed to cover all the exposed surfaces of the figure below? Include surfaces on which the figure is resting. There are no hidden cubes.

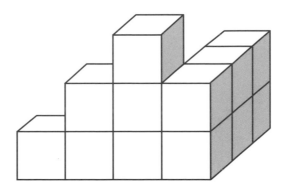

Cast-a-Word

There are 4 dice, and there are different letters of the alphabet on the 6 faces of each of them (each letter appears only once). Random throws of the dice produced the words in this list. Can you figure out which letters appear on each of the 4 dice?

ARCH	GILD	SLOW
BOWL	HARP	TINY
CLAY	JERK	USED
FIVE	MOLE	WALK
FLAN	PITH	ZOIC

Answers on page 180.

Number Sequence

What is the next number in each of the sequences below?

1. 3, 10, 16, 23, 29, ___
   A. 34
   B. 35
   C. 36

2. 5, 10, 15, 30, 45, ___
   A. 90
   B. 50
   C. 60

3. 10, 24, 17, 31, 24, ___
   A. 31
   B. 27
   C. 38

4. 9, 10, 5, 6, 3, ___
   A. 10
   B. 4
   C. 1

Trivia on the Brain

People with the rare disorder "agnosia" (damage to areas of the occipital or parietal brain lobes) can't recognize and identify objects and may not know whether a person's face is familiar to them.

Missing Figure

ANALYSIS　CREATIVE THINKING

Of the figures below (marked A–D), which belongs in the empty grid?

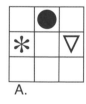 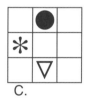 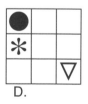

A.　B.　C.　D.

Answer on page 180.

Matchmaker

Use deductive logic to figure out which guy is which, then determine which one belongs to each girl.

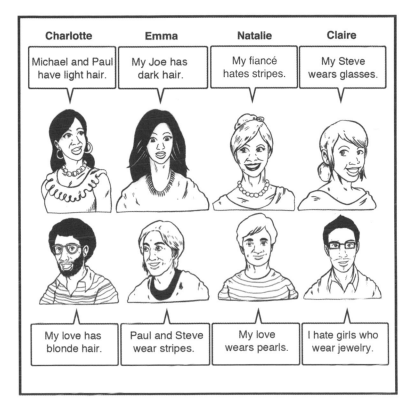

Charlotte
Michael and Paul have light hair.

Emma
My Joe has dark hair.

Natalie
My fiancé hates stripes.

Claire
My Steve wears glasses.

My love has blonde hair.

Paul and Steve wear stripes.

My love wears pearls.

I hate girls who wear jewelry.

Some Change?

If you could only use pennies, nickels, and dimes, what is the minimum number of coins you would need to make $0.38?

Increase the Intensity

Word Jigsaw

LANGUAGE PLANNING

Fit the pieces into the frame to form common words reading across and down. There's no need to rotate the pieces; they'll fit as shown, with each piece used once.

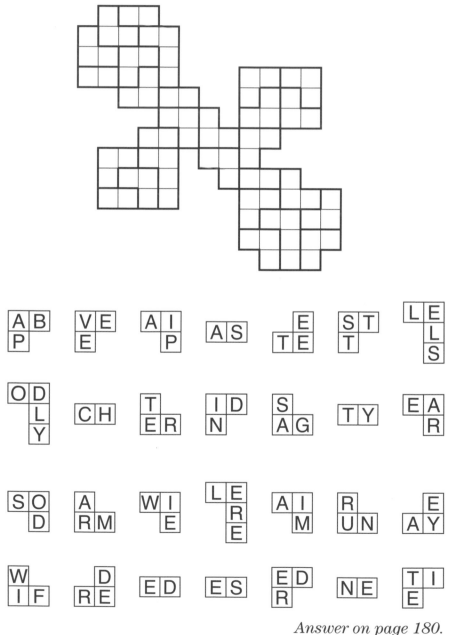

LEVEL 3

Answer on page 180.

Visual Sequence ANALYSIS CREATIVE THINKING

Which of the lettered figures continues the sequence?

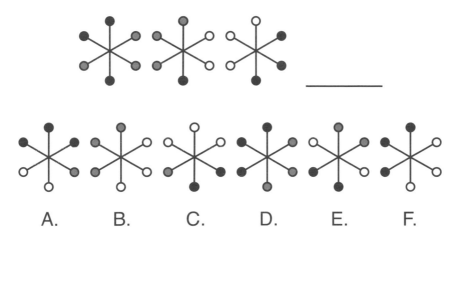

A.   B.   C.   D.   E.   F.

Chain Grid Fill LANGUAGE PLANNING

To complete this puzzle, place the given words into the darkened chains in this grid. Words will run across, down, and diagonally along each darkened chain. It is up to you to figure out which letters go in the single white squares in the grid. When the grid is complete, each column of the grid will contain one of the following words: biting, blenders, checkers, exciting, exotic, notice, panthers, prince, shorts, southern, statue. We filled in one word to get you started.

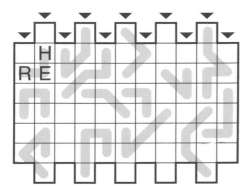

1. BEE, CAT, DOT, NOT

2. HUES, NICK, SEER, SHUT, SOON, TINE, TIRE

3. PAINT, STERN

Detective Work!

ATTENTION VISUAL SEARCH

Oh no! The museum has been raided and left a real mess! The detective has created a list of the museum's most valuable items. Can you find as many of these items as possible and discover which ones have been stolen?

Answers on page 180.

Name That Icon (Part I)

Look at these illustrations of world-famous icons for a minute, then turn the page for a memory challenge.

Name That Icon (Part II) `MEMORY`

(Do not read this until you have read the previous page!)

Check off the icons you saw on the page 91.

___ Empire State Building   ___ Leaning Tower of Pisa

___ Christ over Rio de Janeiro ___ Great Wall of China

___ Pyramids of Egypt   ___ Mount Rushmore

___ Mount Fuji   ___ Eiffel Tower

___ Roman Coliseum   ___ Taj Mahal

___ Big Ben   ___ Sydney Opera House

___ Sphinx at Giza   ___ Niagara Falls

Area Code `ANALYSIS` `LOGIC`

Which letter takes up the smallest area, I, O, or S?

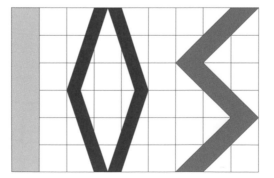

Answers on page 181.

Visualize This!

ANALYSIS LOGIC

On my staircase are many items of clothing. My red sock is above my pants and just below my tie. My right gym shoe is above my tie and immediately below my cowboy hat. My blue sock is below my jacket, which is just below my belt. My jacket is below my white shirt. My white shirt is below my winter coat but immediately below my left gym shoe, which is above my right gym shoe, and also above my cowboy hat. My boxer shorts are lying almost at the top of the stairs, just below my waistcoat. My belt is just below my pants. If I walk up the stairs from the bottom to the top picking up the items, in what order will I collect them?

Cast-a-Word

LOGIC PROBLEM SOLVING

There are 4 dice, and there are different letters of the alphabet on the 6 faces of each of them (each letter appears only once). Random throws of the dice produced the words in this list. Can you figure out which letters appear on each of the 4 dice?

AXIL	HIRE	TAIL
CLUB	PART	TICK
DALE	POSY	WAVE
FAIR	QUIN	WISH
FIRM	SINK	ZONE

CREATIVE THINKING

Cube Fold

SPATIAL VISUALIZATION — VISUAL LOGIC

Below are 5 different perspectives of the same cube. Fill in the 2-dimensional model so that it can be folded up exactly like the cube.

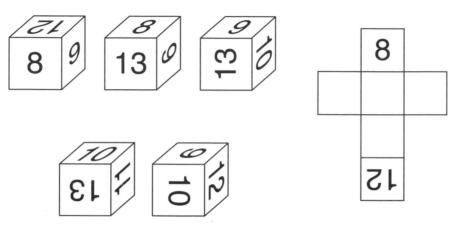

Odd Word Out

ANALYSIS — LOGIC

Which of the words below is the odd one out?

Hint: Think about sounds and meanings.

SITE

HERE

SENT

RIGHT

Answers on page 181.

Fitting Words

In this miniature crossword, the clues are listed randomly and are numbered for convenience only. It is up to you to figure out the placement of the 9 answers. To help you, we've inserted one letter in the grid, and this is the only occurrence of that letter in the completed puzzle.

CLUES

1. Hangs around
2. Hideous
3. Bookie's quote
4. Sidestep
5. Military meal hall
6. Pistol fights
7. "What's the big _____?"
8. Poppy narcotic
9. Sulk

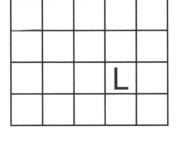

Addagram

This puzzle functions exactly like an anagram (a word that is a rearrangement of another word) with an added step: In addition to being scrambled, each phrase below is missing the same letter. Discover the missing letter, then unscramble the letters. When you do, you'll reveal a recluse, a precious stone, a naval rank, and an unintelligent person.

THEIR

DEALER

RADIAL

AROUSING

Number Cross

Use each of the numbers listed here to complete this clue-less crossword grid. The puzzle has only one solution.

3 FIGURES
152

193

223

247

428

444

452

492

4 FIGURES
1641

1842

2507

3334

3555

4019

4251

4421

5 FIGURES
10727

11722

13122

13452	43810	251486
15461	47453	269437
16429	48578	274742
25730	**6 FIGURES**	294947
28632	111964	337110
30201	123465	378638
30203	143262	418113
32605	152808	440387
41530	153418	462954
42113	222926	

Answer on page 181.

Analogies

Study the relationships of the word pairs to discover what's missing.

1. Radio is to television as VHS is to _____.
   A. DVD
   B. VCR
   C. Blu-ray

2. Novel is to chapter as unit is to _____.
   A. city
   B. structure
   C. complex

3. Artist is to critic as _____ is to judge.
   A. criminal
   B. beauty
   C. court

4. Gem is to diamond as animal is to _____.
   A. vegetable
   B. species
   C. cow

Meeting Point

Alice and Ben are walking toward each other. Ben is walking faster, but he is walking uphill while Alice is walking downhill. Who will reach their meeting point first?

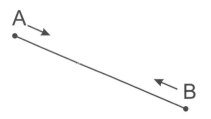

CREATIVE THINKING

Paper Cut

SPATIAL VISUALIZATION VISUAL LOGIC

Imagine a circle cut out of a piece of paper. Fold it in half as in
Figure 2. Fold it again as in Figure 3. Then cut the tips off of each of
the 3 corners as shown in Figure 4. If you were then to unfold the
piece of paper, would it look like A, B, C, or D?

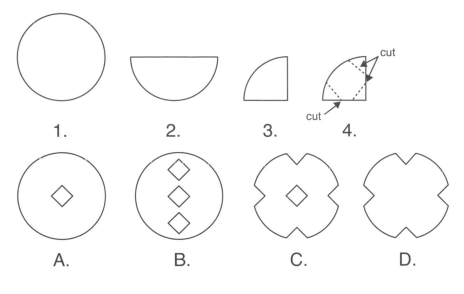

1.   2.   3.   4.

A.   B.   C.   D.

Add-a-Word

ANALYSIS LANGUAGE

Add one word to each of the 3-word sets to create new words or
phrases. For example: In a set including "smith," "fore," and "game,"
the added word would be "word" (creating "wordsmith," "foreword,"
and "word game").

1. Couch, chip, sweet: _____

2. Mill, bell, mint: _____

3. Seat, second, split: _____

4. Pole, green, bag: _____

5. Dome, skin, yellow: _____

6. Paper, paddy, wild: _____

Answers on page 181.

Quipu

Which of the 3 Quipus (Incan devices for recording information) is identical to the one in the frame? Quipus are considered identical when they can be matched perfectly only by rotating pieces around the knots—they cannot be lifted or turned over. See the examples for further clarification.

EXAMPLE 1 **EXAMPLE 2**

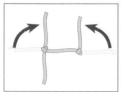 

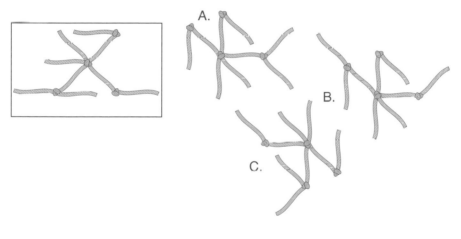

Arrows (Part I)

Study the image below for 10 seconds, then wait one minute before turning the page for a memory challenge.

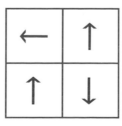

Arrows (Part II)

LEVEL 3

(Do not read this until you have read the previous page!)

Which one of the following groupings did you see on page 99?

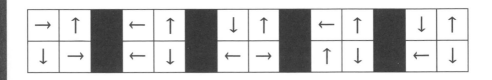

What Comes Next?

ANALYSIS

CREATIVE THINKING

Study the series of letters below. Every letter in each series is the first letter of a word, and all the words in each series are related. For example, if the first 4 letters of a series were M, V, E, M, they could stand for Mercury, Venus, Earth, and Mars. Logically, the next letter would be J, for Jupiter.

Continue each series below by discovering the next logical word.

  1. E, G, B, D, ___

  2. H, O, M, E, ___

  3. P, N, D, Q, H, ___

Answers on page 181.

Quilt Quest

The small, tricolored shape on the right appears 3 times in the quilt below. Find all 3 instances. The shape can be rotated but not mirrored.

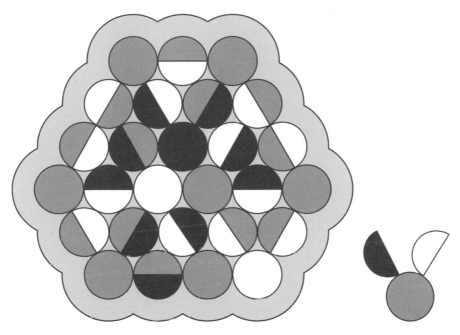

Odd Word Out

One of the words below does not belong with the others based on a straightforward reason. Which is the odd word out?

feedback

boldface

embraced

backside

cupboard

abdicate

Brothers and Sisters ANALYSIS LOGIC

L
E
V
E
L

3

Use deductive logic to determine the name of each guy, then figure out which girl is his sister.

Word Spiral LANGUAGE

Scrambled in the box below is a common word. **L** is its first letter. What is the word?

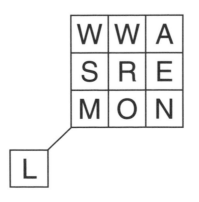

Answers on page 182.

From 0 to 100

Which digit (from 0 to 9) appears with the least amount of frequency between 0 and 100?

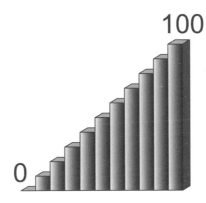

Visual Sequence ANALYSIS CREATIVE THINKING

Which of the lettered figures continues the sequence?

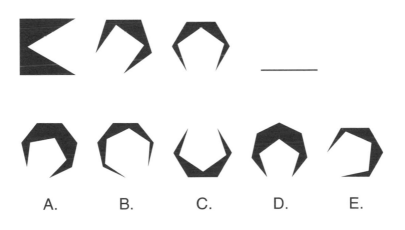

A.　　B.　　C.　　D.　　E.

Knot Problem

Which hook(s) should be removed to make the picture fall to the ground?

Cast-a-Word

There are 4 dice, and there are different letters of the alphabet on the 6 faces of each of them (each letter appears only once). Random throws of the dice produced the words in this list. Can you figure out which letters appear on each of the 4 dice?

AXIS	FURY	LING
BAIL	GLAD	SACK
BREW	HOPE	SLIP
CASE	JOLT	STUN
COWL	JURY	VINO
DAZE		

Answers on page 182.

Pattern Placement

CREATIVE THINKING

SPATIAL VISUALIZATION | VISUAL LOGIC

When meshed together, which 3 patterns (marked A–F) can form the grid shown in the center? Patterns cannot be rotated or flipped.

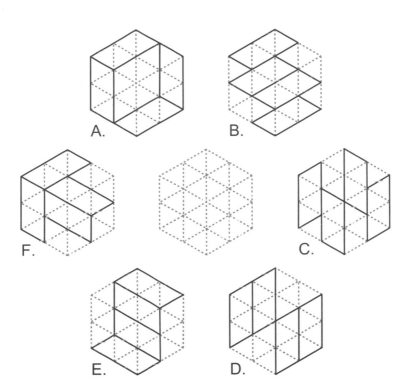

A.

B.

F.

C.

E.

D.

Trivia on the Brain

If your diet includes healthy portions of produce, fish, nuts, and vinaigrette-type dressings, you could cut your risk of Alzheimer's disease by 42 percent!

Answer on page 182.

Cube Fold

Below is an unfolded cube. Only 2 of the cubes below (marked A–E) can possibly represent this cube when folded. Which 2?

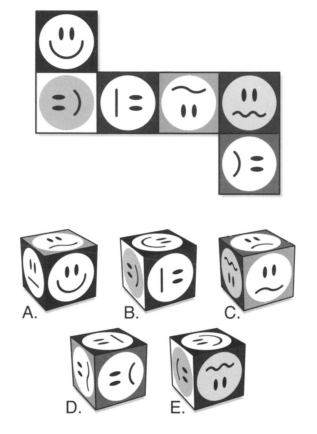

A.   B.   C.

D.   E.

What Type?

COMPUTATION   PROBLEM SOLVING

If 2 typists can type 2 pages in 5 minutes, how many typists does it take to type 20 pages in 10 minutes?

    A. 5   B. 10   C. 15   D. 20

Answers on page 182.

Not Exactly! (Part I)

Read the following text—paying close attention—before turning the page for a memory challenge.

Ever notice that some words don't mean what they seem to be saying?

For instance, take your common everyday eggplants. They seem to be missing something—like eggs!

If you happen to be first on the scene after an airplane crash, don't waste too much time looking for the "black box." It's bright orange, to make it easier to locate in wreckage.

Guinea pigs don't come from New Guinea (they originated in the Andes). And oh yeah, they're not pigs. (They're rodents.) One wonders if they ever hang out with koala bears, which are not really bears. (They're marsupials.)

The Underground Railroad wasn't underground, nor was it a railroad. It was a network of escape routes to help fugitive slaves reach freedom safely.

Sticks of chalk are no longer made of chalk but of gypsum.

Ever notice that pineapples don't contain pine, or apples?

We hope these tickle your funny bone. Which, of course, is not an actual bone—it's your ulnar nerve.

Trivia on the Brain
Most people can memorize a maximum of 300,000 facts over the course of a lifetime.

Not Exactly! (Part II)

MEMORY

(Do not read this until you have read the previous page!)

Based on the information you read on page 107, answer the following questions:

1. Where did Guinea pigs originate?

2. If koala bears aren't bears, what are they?

3. If your funny bone isn't a bone, what is it?

4. What color is an airplane's "black box"?

5. What are sticks of chalk made of?

Fitting Words

GENERAL KNOWLEDGE / PLANNING

In this miniature crossword, the clues are listed randomly and are numbered for convenience only. It is up to you to figure out the placement of the 9 answers. To help you, we've inserted one letter in the grid, and this is the only occurrence of that letter in the completed puzzle.

CLUES

1. District
2. Flying solo
3. Word following "abs of" or "stainless"
4. Touched down
5. Film holder
6. Chop finely, as onions
7. St. Louis football team
8. First word of "The Raven"
9. Barber's tool

Answers on page 182.

How Many?

How many rectangles can you count in this shape?

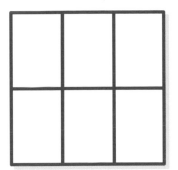

Add-a-Word

Add one word to each of the 3-word sets to create new words or phrases. For example: In a set including "smith," "fore," and "game," the added word would be "word" (creating "wordsmith," "foreword," and "word game").

1. box, fox, gold: _____

2. air, battle, day: _____

3. pay, off, data: _____

4. ding, man, boy: _____

5. eye, gum, room: _____

6. dream, mate, work: _____

Answers on pages 182–183.

Letter Logic

L E V E L 3

Use each of the words, names, and acronyms listed here to complete this clue-less crossword grid. The puzzle has only one solution.

3 LETTERS
AGA
ALL

4 LETTERS
HERO
IONS
KING
MAZE
OATH
OMEN
PARK
POLO
SOUP
SPOT
TEAL
TUBA

5 LETTERS
ACUTE
BRACE
CATCH
DITCH
FIERY
FLAME
LADEN
LEARN
MAUVE
MOTET
MOTOR
NERVE

OZONE
PATIO
PHONY
PROSE
RANCH
REACH
RIOJA
ROAST

ROOST
SURGE

6 LETTERS
CLOUDY
ESTEEM
MENACE
PANTRY

ROCKET
SEQUEL

7 LETTERS
AMNESTY
CARTOON
DISSECT
LESSONS

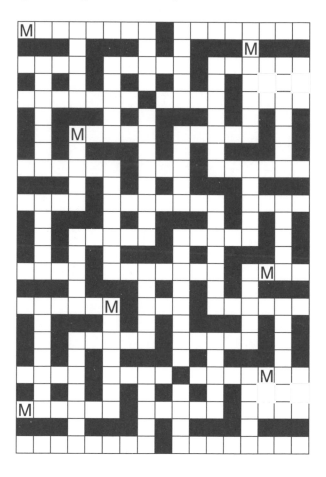

Answer on page 183.

LUGGAGE SARDINE **8 LETTERS** PINNACLE
MIDWIFE SOLOMON ANTELOPE TREASURY
PIONEER STUDENT DEMOLISH
PRALINE TITANIC KANGAROO
ROUTINE UNARMED MARMOSET

LEVEL 3

A Passion for Fashion (Part I)

`MEMORY`

Study these wearable items for a minute, then turn the page for a memory challenge.

Tank top

Platform shoes

Bell-bottoms

Cargo pants

Ball gown

Turtleneck sweater

Overalls

Pearls

A Passion for Fashion (Part II)

`MEMORY`

(Do not read this until you have read the previous page!)

Check off the items you saw on page 111.

___ Mao jacket

___ Camisole

___ Tank top

___ Overalls

___ Capri pants

___ Bolero jacket

___ Bell-bottoms

___ Earrings

___ Platform shoes

___ Bermuda shorts

___ Turtleneck sweater

___ Miniskirt

___ Cargo pants

___ Tube top

Dissection

`CREATIVE THINKING`
`SPATIAL VISUALIZATION` `VISUAL LOGIC`

Separate the figure into 5 identical parts following the grid lines. The parts may be rotated and/or mirrored.

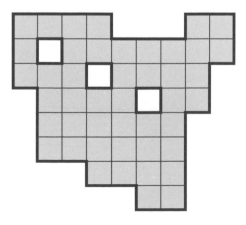

Answers on page 183.

Curve Fill

COMPUTATION PLANNING

Fill in each heavy-outlined set of cells with the same number (0, 2, or 5) so that the sums given for each curved row and column and the 2 sections extending from the center oval are true. For further insight, see the example puzzle.

EXAMPLE

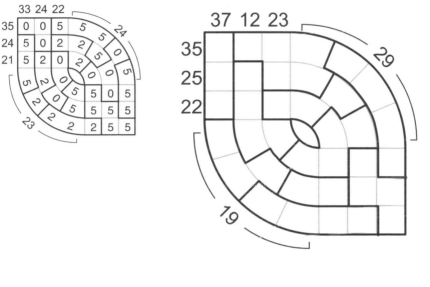

Number Sequence

ANALYSIS
CREATIVE THINKING

What fraction comes next?

$$\frac{1}{5}, \ \frac{1}{3}, \ \frac{1}{7}, \ \frac{1}{5}, \ \frac{1}{9}, \ \frac{1}{7}, \ \frac{1}{11}, \ \frac{1}{9}, \ \frac{1}{13}, \ \frac{1}{11}, \ \_\_\_$$

A. $\frac{1}{7}$ B. $\frac{1}{13}$ C. $\frac{1}{15}$ D. $\frac{1}{11}$

Word Jigsaw

Fit the pieces into the frame to form common words reading across and down. There's no need to rotate the pieces; they'll fit as shown, with each piece used once.

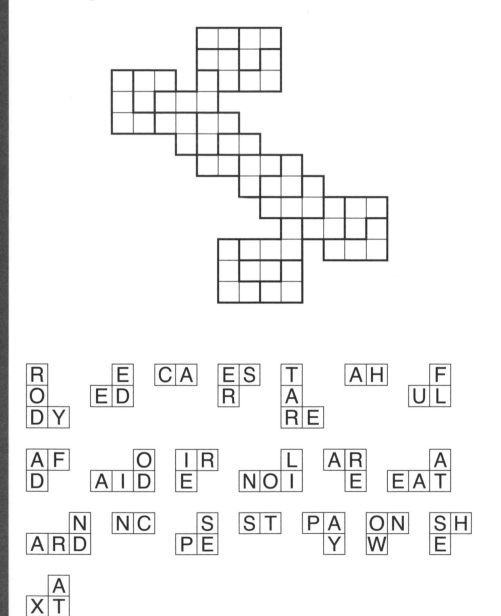

Answer on page 183.

Cube Count

In the 3-dimensional cube shown below, how many of the individual squares are completely hidden from view inside the cube?

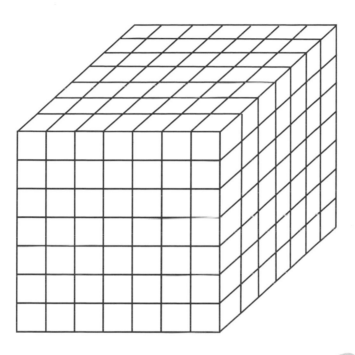

Trivia on the Brain

Some may claim to have a photographic memory, but most scientists are pretty convinced such a thing doesn't exist. Studies have shown that certain people are able to train their brains to remember things well, but humans as a whole tend to have poor memories. In fact, of the 3 creatures that are able to remember the way they look in a mirror—the orangutan, the dolphin, and the human—only we can turn around and instantly forget what our own faces look like.

Answer on page 183.   115

L
E
V
E
L

3

Number Sequence

What is the next number in each of the sequences below?

1. 8, 16, 12, 24, 18, ___
   A. 10
   B. 36
   C. 26

2. 4, 20, 10, 50, 25, ___
   A. 125
   B. 75
   C. 100

3. 1, 7, 8, 15, 23, ___
   A. 31
   B. 24
   C. 38

4. 12, 13, 25, 26, 51, ___
   A. 63
   B. 52
   C. 77

Trivia on the Brain

The probability that a person might forget his or her own name is about the same as that of getting hit by an asteroid: It could happen, but it's not very likely.

Answers on page 183.

How to Survive an Arctic Night (Part I)

Read the following text—paying close attention—before turning the page for a memory challenge.

Could you survive overnight in a field of Arctic snow if you didn't have a shelter? Yes, if you knew how to build an igloo.

An Inuit can build one of these remarkable dome shelters in about an hour.

He uses a snow knife, which is similar to a machete. Its blade is about as wide as a sword blade but not as long.

The first step is to draw a circle on the ground the size of the igloo. Then, working from inside, cut blocks of snow from the ground to build the shelter. The snow must be easy to pack, not dry and powdery. Form a circular row of large blocks. As the walls are built up, stack the blocks in toward the center slightly to help form a dome shape.

The last piece is the block of snow that will form the cap at the top. Then a hole is poked through the top for ventilation. Any spaces or open cracks in the walls are filled with snow.

Finally a small door or entranceway is carved for going in and out, and a chunk of snow is cut and kept next to the door. You'll use it to block the door to keep the cold out when you're ready to be inside for the night.

Even with the temperature outside at 45 degrees below zero (Fahrenheit), the temperature inside an igloo will range from about 20 to 60 degrees above, just from body heat.

How to Survive an Arctic Night (Part II)

MEMORY

(Do not look at this until you have read the previous page!)

Based on the information you read on page 117, answer the following questions:

1. What is the temperature inside an igloo?

2. What is the basic tool for building an igloo?

3. What other tool is a snow knife similar to?

4. Why do you poke a hole in the top?

5. What natural heat source warms the igloo?

Hidden Word

ANALYSIS **LOGIC**

Hidden below is a common word. Unscramble the letters to discover what it is.

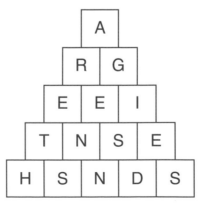

Answers on page 183.

Number Cross

Use each of the numbers listed here to complete this clue-less crossword grid. The puzzle has only one solution.

3 FIGURES

131

143

240

252

261

265

335

351

4 FIGURES

1313

1665

2265

2626

3132

3146

3424

3610

5 FIGURES

10162

10263

12225

12263

13121

13212

16666

21226

22130

24201

24466

30522

33024

33134

33632

34445

6 FIGURES

111562

115316

122404

135113

151231

165656

214064

220600

224065

235242

240105

253056

335332

335403

356666

Answer on page 184.

Cube Fold

CREATIVE THINKING

SPATIAL VISUALIZATION   VISUAL LOGIC

Below are 5 different sides of a solid object constructed out of several identical cubes fused together. What does the sixth side look like?

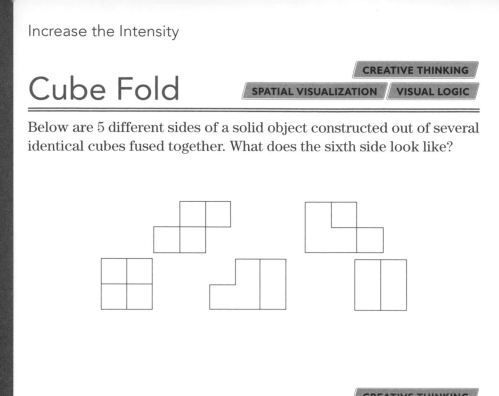

Quilt Quest

CREATIVE THINKING

SPATIAL VISUALIZATION   VISUAL LOGIC

The small, tricolored shape on the right appears 3 times in the quilt below. Find all 3 instances. The shape can be rotated but not mirrored.

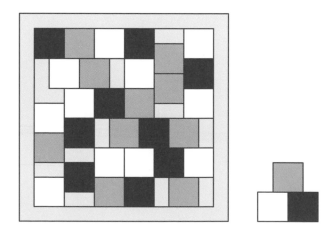

Answers on page 184.

Character Substitute

Which character should be in place of the question mark below?

! # % & ?

Quipu

Which of the 3 Quipus (Incan devices for recording information) is identical to the one in the frame? Quipus are considered identical when they can be matched perfectly only by rotating pieces around the knots—they cannot be lifted or turned over. See the examples for further clarification.

EXAMPLE 1   **EXAMPLE 2**

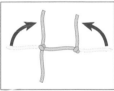

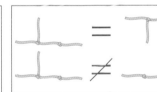

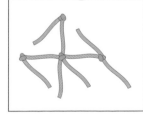

A.

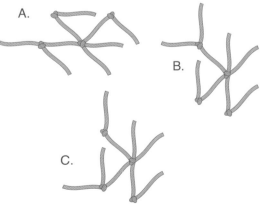

B.

C.

Analogies

CREATIVE THINKING   GENERAL KNOWLEDGE

Study the relationships of the word pairs to discover what's missing.

1. Cow is to bull as hen is to _____.
   A. chick
   B. chicken
   C. rooster

2. Peeved is to furious as pleased is to _____.
   A. delighted
   B. angry
   C. thankful

3. Downpour is to flood as earthquake is to _____.
   A. tsunami
   B. tornado
   C. fault line

4. Sad is to blue as embarrassed is to _____.
   A. humiliated
   B. red
   C. greed

Trivia on the Brain

The brain does funny things when we sleep, including propelling us to perform somnambulism (sleepwalking) and somniloquy (sleeptalking).

Answers on page 184.

Pythagorize It!

Blacken one white dot within the board so that from this dot exactly 4 symmetrical squares can be drawn. Squares must be drawn along the black dots. See the example illustration for clarification.

EXAMPLE

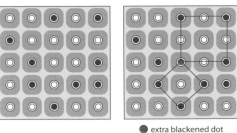

● extra blackened dot

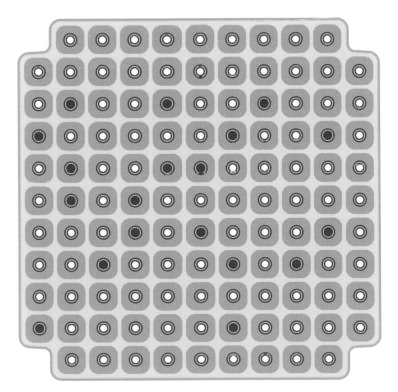

Answer on page 184.

Cube Fold

Below is an unfolded cube. Only 2 of the cubes below (marked A–E) can possibly represent this cube when folded. Which 2?

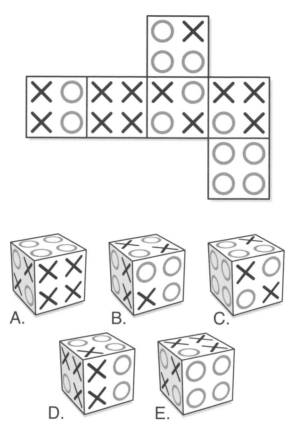

A.   B.   C.

D.   E.

Anagram

What do you get when you combine and unscramble these 2 words: REGAIN TAN?

        A. A city

        B. A world-famous landmark

        C. A country

        D. A river

Answers on page 184.

Curve Fill

Fill in each heavy-outlined set of cells with the same number (0, 2, or 5) so that the sums given for each curved row and column and the 2 sections extending from the center oval are true. For further insight, see the example puzzle.

EXAMPLE

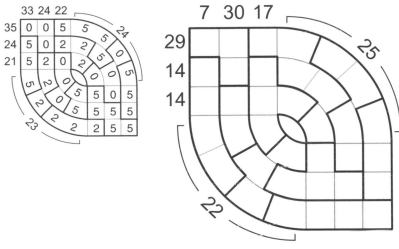

Add-a-Word

ANALYSIS LANGUAGE

Add one word to each of the 3-word sets to create new words or phrases. For example: In a set including "smith," "fore," and "game," the added word would be "word" (creating "wordsmith," "foreword," and "word game").

1. rail, hog, rage: _____

2. easy, car, back: _____

3. war, foot, finder: _____

4. cat, blind, way: _____

5. fertile, moon, red: _____

6. mix, paper, blaze: _____

Answers on page 184.

Figure Trace

ANALYSIS LOGIC

Can you re-create the figure below without lifting the pencil, retracing, or crossing any lines? It must be created in one continuous movement of the pencil.

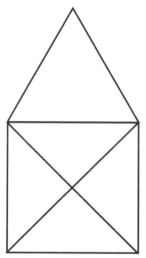

Letter-In

ANALYSIS LOGIC

What letter should replace the question mark below?

Answers on page 185.

Pattern
Recognition

Based on the logical pattern established in the number sets below, what number should replace the question mark in the last set?

A. 1   B. 15   C. 20   D. 21

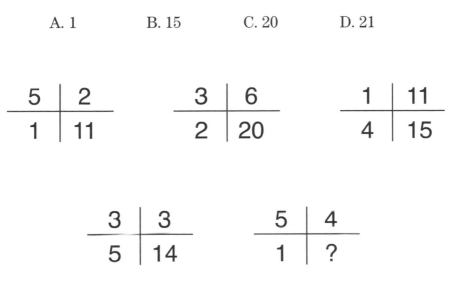

$$\begin{array}{c|c} 5 & 2 \\ \hline 1 & 11 \end{array} \qquad \begin{array}{c|c} 3 & 6 \\ \hline 2 & 20 \end{array} \qquad \begin{array}{c|c} 1 & 11 \\ \hline 4 & 15 \end{array}$$

$$\begin{array}{c|c} 3 & 3 \\ \hline 5 & 14 \end{array} \qquad \begin{array}{c|c} 5 & 4 \\ \hline 1 & ? \end{array}$$

Trivia on the Brain

Researchers think that the mental capacity of a 100-year-old person who has perfect memory could be represented by a computer with 10 to the power of 15 bits (one petabit). At the rate technology is growing today, that figure will probably be attainable in about 35 years. One caveat: This only represents memory capacity, not thought creation or emotions, which are extremely complex.

Answer on page 185.

Go the Distance

A Musical Discovery

LOGIC

Scholars recently unearthed a folio of previously unknown sonatas written in the 19th century by a composer known only as "Z." His real name is lost to history, but we know that he worked on his music only for a period of 5 years between 1863 and 1867 and that he had the habit of naming his compositions after women he admired. This new folio contained 5 sonatas, each of a different type (flute, piano, violin, etc.) and each in a different key (A minor, C major, etc.). It was no surprise to anyone that each sonata was named after a different woman. Using only the clues below, determine the type, title, and key of each sonata, as well as the year in which "Z" composed it.

Year	Title	Instrument	Key
1863			
1864			
1865			
1866			
1867			

1. The earliest of the 5 sonatas was in either C minor or D minor.

2. *Margot* was composed one year before the sonata in C major, which wasn't named *Eliza*.

3. Of *Heloise* and the clarinet sonata (which wasn't the earliest of the 5 pieces), one was in D minor and the other was composed in 1865.

4. The piano sonata wasn't in the key of C minor.

5. Either the flute sonata or the one composed in 1864 was in C major.

6. The 1865 sonata was titled either *Theresa* or *Heloise*.

7. The 1866 cello sonata, which was named after the infamous Lady Margot Winthorpe, wasn't in A minor.

8. Neither *Beatrice* nor the C major sonata was written in 1863.

9. *Beatrice* was composed one year after the violin sonata.

		Title					Instrument					Key				
		Beatrice	Eliza	Heloise	Margot	Theresa	Cello	Clarinet	Flute	Piano	Violin	A minor	C major	C minor	D minor	E minor
Year	1863															
	1864															
	1865															
	1866															
	1867															
Key	A minor															
	C major															
	C minor															
	D minor															
	E minor															
Instrument	Cello															
	Clarinet															
	Flute															
	Piano															
	Violin															

Hitori

PLANNING **VISUAL LOGIC**

The object of this puzzle is to have a number appear only once in each row and column. By shading a number cell, you are effectively removing that number from its row and column. There's a catch though: Shaded number cells are never adjacent to one another in a row or column.

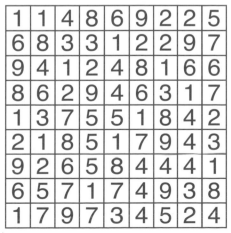

Animal Phrasing

ATTENTION **VISUAL SEARCH**

Find 7 pairs of images in this picture that form phrases containing the name of an animal. For example: An image of an alley and a cat would give you "alley cat."

Answers on page 185.

Triangular Sums

Can you place the numbers 1 through 9 around the triangle so that no 2 consecutive numbers are together and each side has a sum of 17? There are 2 ways to do this.

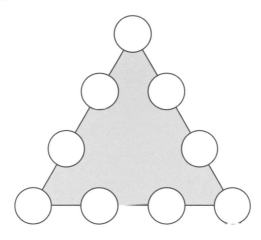

Add-a-Word

Add one word to each of the 3-word sets to create new words or phrases. For example: In a set including "smith," "fore," and "game," the added word would be "word" (creating "wordsmith," "foreword," and "word game").

1. sticks, second, bass: _____

2. time, dive, shell: _____

3. train, silver, proof: _____

4. head, root, broken: _____

5. range, air, butt: _____

6. dance, broad, play: _____

L E V E L 4

Overlapping Sheets

CREATIVE THINKING

SPATIAL VISUALIZATION | **VISUAL LOGIC**

What is the smallest number of square sheets of paper, all the same size, that can be placed over each other to form this figure?

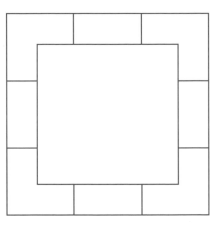

Visualize This!

ANALYSIS | **LOGIC**

I am walking down a road filled with many landmarks. After crossing a bridge I must climb over a fence, but not before I cross the aqueduct. The restaurant I pass is farther than the signpost before the bridge, with 5 other landmarks in between. The signpost lies at the bottom of a great hill, and the bridge is located immediately after the signpost. The final landmark is not the canal lock, and it isn't between the signpost and the restaurant. The wishing well and the scarecrow are the last 2 landmarks before the restaurant. The traffic lights are not found near the beginning of the list, and have but one landmark adjacent to them. The other 2 landmarks in question are a ditch and a crossroads, the latter of which does not begin the list but is located before the hill. In what order do I encounter these landmarks on my journey?

Answers on pages 185–186.

Word Jigsaw

Fit the pieces into the frame to form common words reading across and down. There's no need to rotate the pieces; they'll fit as shown, with each piece used once.

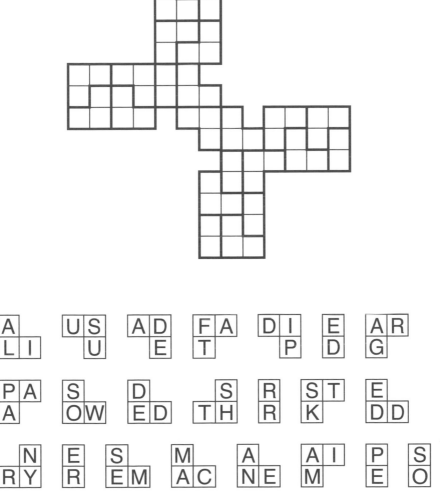

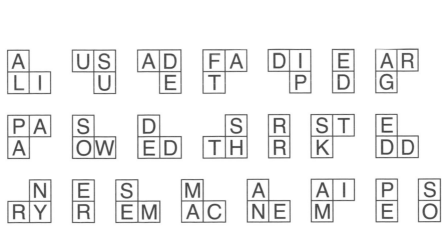

L
E
V
E
L

4

LEVEL 4

Odd One Out

CREATIVE THINKING

SPATIAL VISUALIZATION   VISUAL LOGIC

Which figure is the odd one out?

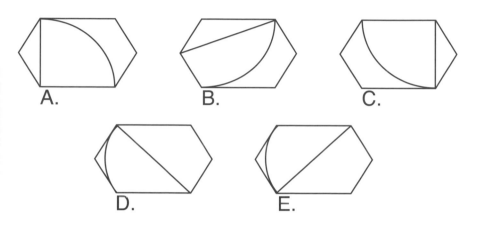

A.

B.

C.

D.

E.

Game Time

ANALYSIS   LOGIC

Study these football scores:

Oklahoma 10   Baylor 7

Minnesota 35   Baylor 3

Nebraska 14   Oklahoma 10

If Minnesota were to play Oklahoma, based on these results, they would:

A. Lose by 15

B. Lose by 29

C. Win by 15

D. Win by 29

Answers on page 186.

Visual Sequence

Which of the lettered figures continues the sequence?

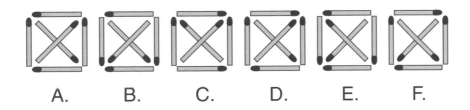

A. B. C. D. E. F.

Mini-Cross (Part I)

Solve this small crossword, then turn the page for a memory challenge.

ACROSS

1. Large parrot
6. Informed
7. Steers, as a ship
8. Mix of rain and snow

DOWN

1. PC alternatives
2. GI who hasn't reported in
3. Mr. Peanut accessory
4. "Rule, Britannia" composer
5. Direction outlaws go

1.	2.	3.	4.	5.
6.				
7.				
8.				

Answers on page 186. 135

Mini-Cross (Part II)

MEMORY

(Do not read this until you have solved the puzzle on the previous page!)

Check off the words that appeared in the solved puzzle on page 135.

___ Parakeet   ___ AWOL

___ Aware   ___ Top hat

___ Fleet   ___ Cane

___ West   ___ East

___ Toucan   ___ Macaw

     ___ Macs

Cast-a-Word

LOGIC   PROBLEM SOLVING

There are 4 dice, and there are different letters of the alphabet on the 6 faces of each of them (each letter appears only once). Random throws of the dice produced the words in this list. Can you figure out which letters appear on each of the 4 dice?

ALTO	FLEA	OVER
BAPS	HULK	PONY
BLOW	IOTA	QUIZ
DREG	JACK	STAG
ECHO	LAZE	TYPO

Answers on page 186.

Chain Grid Fill

LANGUAGE | PLANNING

To complete this puzzle, place the given words into the darkened chains in this grid. Words will run across, down, and diagonally along each darkened chain. It is up to you to figure out which letters go in the single white squares in the grid. When the grid is complete, each column of the grid will contain one of the following words: crayon, cyclones, digger, Mexico, pencil, public, spatulas, thinking, time zone, turnover, tuxedo. We filled in one word to get you started.

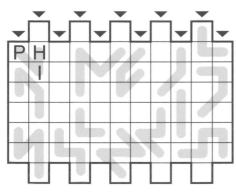

1. EGG, LID, PUT, ZOO

2. BUNK, DONE, MATE, ONCE, RENO

3. ICING, LIVER, LOANS, PRIME

Addagram

LANGUAGE

This puzzle functions exactly like an anagram (a word that is a rearrangement of another word) with an added step: In addition to being scrambled, each phrase below is missing the same letter. Discover the missing letter, then unscramble the letters. When you do, you'll reveal a root vegetable, a bowman, an adhesive sea creature, and a word meaning "relevant."

INPUT

REACH

BALANCE

PENITENT

Answers on page 186.

CREATIVE THINKING

Cube Fold

SPATIAL VISUALIZATION | VISUAL LOGIC

Below is an unfolded cube. Only 2 of the cubes below (marked A–E) can possibly represent this cube when folded. Which 2?

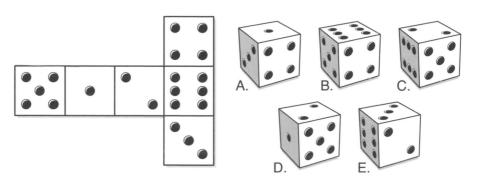

Fitting Words

GENERAL KNOWLEDGE | PLANNING

In this miniature crossword, the clues are listed randomly and are numbered for convenience only. It is up to you to figure out the placement of the 9 answers. To help you, we've inserted one letter in the grid, and this is the only occurrence of that letter in the completed puzzle.

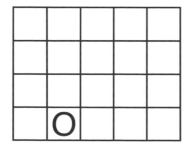

CLUES

1. Excessive
2. Homophone of the answer to clue 1 that means "release"
3. Campus hangout
4. Dominate
5. Prescribed amounts
6. Motor oil purchase
7. Driving aids
8. Tosses in
9. To confuse

Answers on page 186.

Knot Problem

Which 2 pieces of string are linked together, A or B? Study the example below for help on linked and unlinked string. The figure on the left is unlinked; the figure on the right is linked.

EXAMPLE

A.

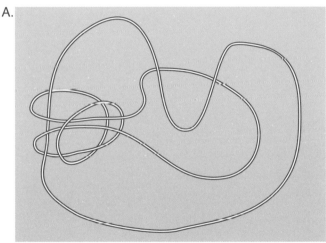

B.

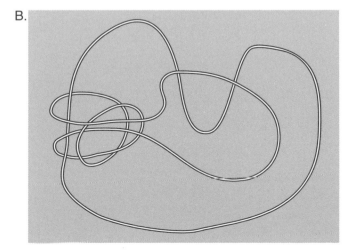

Answer on page 186. 139

Triangular Pattern

CREATIVE THINKING

SPATIAL VISUALIZATION   VISUAL LOGIC

The letters on the vertices of the triangles below form a logical pattern. According to that pattern, what letter should replace the question mark in the last triangle?

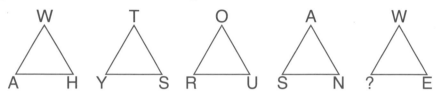

Quilt Quest

CREATIVE THINKING

SPATIAL VISUALIZATION   VISUAL LOGIC

The small, tricolored shape on the right appears twice in the quilt below. Find both instances. The shape can be rotated but not mirrored.

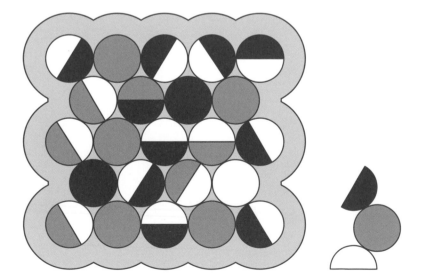

Answers on page 187.

Which Dog Is Mine?

Use deductive logic to figure out which dog is which and who owns which dog?

Pop Quiz

GENERAL KNOWLEDGE

One of the following is the "odd man out." Which one?

A. Koala bear

B. Kangaroo

C. Wombat

D. Possum

E. Anteater

Number Cross

ANALYSIS **PLANNING**

Use each of the numbers listed below to complete this clue-less crossword grid. The puzzle has only one solution.

3 FIGURES

145

156

241

253

262

301

304

363

4 FIGURES

2203

Column 1	Column 2	Column 3	Column 4
2410	23130	34532	165232
2426	23145	35133	232162
2560	23602	36343	232365
3362	24121	36624	235104
3535	24263	**6 FIGURES**	253524
3541	25240	102340	322420
3602	26403	142206	325123
	30121	142322	332363
5 FIGURES	34053	142335	355500
10263	34255	163646	363535
12363			

Answer on page 187.

Odd One Out

Which shape doesn't belong?

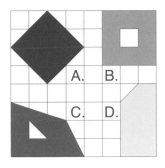

Quipu

Which 2 of the 3 Quipus (Incan devices for recording information) is identical to the one in the frame? Quipus are considered identical when they can be matched perfectly only by rotating pieces around the knots—they cannot be lifted or turned over. See the examples for further clarification.

EXAMPLE 1   **EXAMPLE 2**

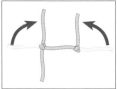

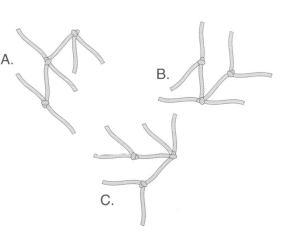

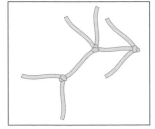

Missing Number `ANALYSIS` `COMPUTATION`

A certain logic determines the number in the middle of each diamond. What number replaces the question mark in figure F?

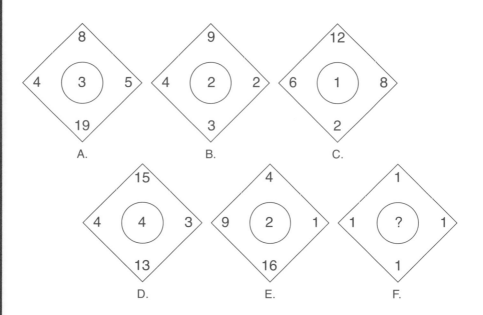

A.   B.   C.

D.   E.   F.

Trivia on the Brain

Scientists have found that it is impossible to learn something well enough to create a "permanent" memory; all memories have a limited lifetime.

Answer on page 187.

What Comes Next?

Study the series of letters below. Every letter in each series is the first letter of a word, and all the words in each series are related. For example, if the first 4 letters of a series were M, V, E, M, they could stand for Mercury, Venus, Earth, and Mars. Logically, the next letter would be J, for Jupiter.

Continue each series below by discovering the next logical word.

1. G, A, A, D, E, A, ____

2. R, O, Y, G, B, I, ____

3. F, S, T, F, F, S, ____

Game Board (Part I)

MEMORY

Study this game board for a minute, particularly the shapes and their placement. Then, turn the page for a memory challenge.

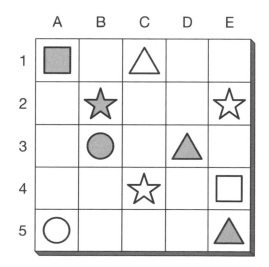

Game Board (Part II)

MEMORY

(Do not read this until you have read the previous page!)

Duplicate the board as seen on page 145.

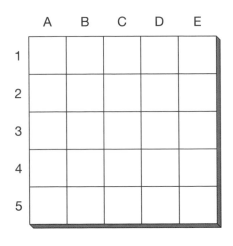

Chain Grid Fill

LANGUAGE   PLANNING

To complete this puzzle, place the given words into the darkened chains in this grid. Words will run across, down, and diagonally along each darkened chain. It is up to you to figure out which letters go in the single white squares in the grid. When the grid is complete, each column of the grid will contain one of the following words: bankrupt, Buddhist, bureau, charge, composed, Klondike, Passover, potato, steamy, stogie, yodels. We filled in one word to get you started.

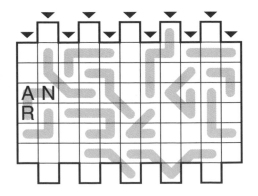

1. AIM, BAY, DIG, NOD, TOE

2. LURK, MOTH, POOL, POST, USER

3. GOATS, PASTE, SYRUP

Answers on pages 187–188.

Missing Figure

Which figure completes this sequence?

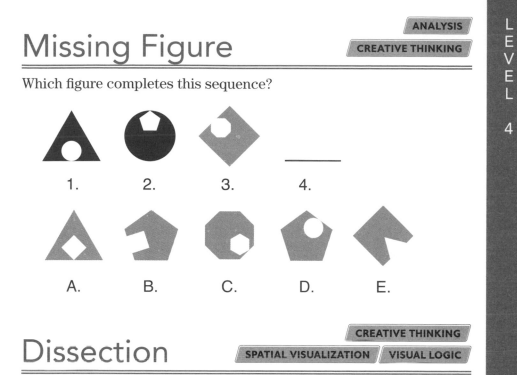

1.   2.   3.   4.

A.   B.   C.   D.   E.

Dissection

Separate the figure into 2 identical parts following the grid lines. The parts may be rotated and/or mirrored.

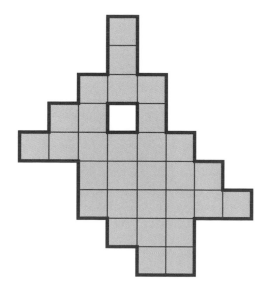

Knot Problem

CREATIVE THINKING

SPATIAL VISUALIZATION | VISUAL LOGIC

If we pull the 2 upper loops of the pieces of string as shown in the diagram, which one will produce a knot?

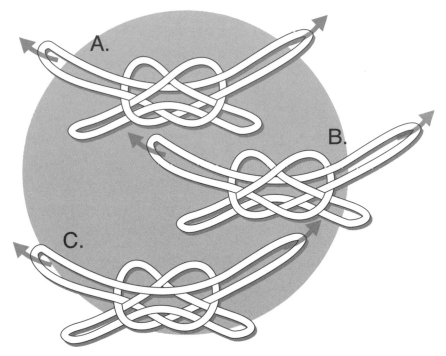

A.

B.

C.

Trivia on the Brain

The Greek philosopher Aristotle believed that the heart, not the brain, was the seat of mental processes. Most people agreed, which is where the term "memorize by heart" comes from.

Answer on page 188.

Cube Fold

Below is an unfolded cube. Only 2 of the cubes below (marked A–E) can possibly represent this cube when folded. Which 2?

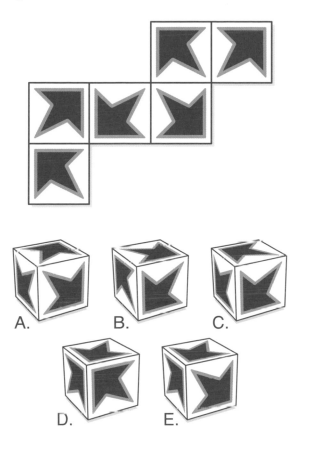

A.   B.   C.

D.   E.

One of These Things. . .

One of these numbers does not belong with the others based on a simple reason. Which is the odd one out?

A. 19370   B. 88112   C. 56045

D. 43346   E. 38524   F. 75152

Answers on page 188.   149

Pattern Placement

CREATIVE THINKING

SPATIAL VISUALIZATION   VISUAL LOGIC

When meshed together, which 3 patterns below (marked A–F) can form the grid shown in the center? Patterns cannot be rotated or flipped.

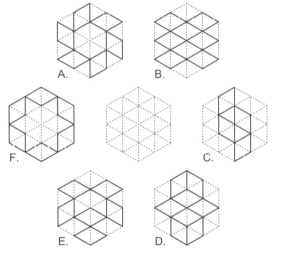

Grid Fill

LANGUAGE   PLANNING

To complete this puzzle, place the given letters and words into the shapes in this grid. Words and letters will run across, down, and wrap around each shape. When the grid is filled, each row will contain one of the following words: access, aching, cloths, erodes, kettle, league, sprint.

1. L, S, T

2. AG, SS, TI

3. ACE, ODE, SUE

4. ETCH, LORE, SACK

5. LENGTH, PRINCE

Answers on page 188.

Fitting Words

GENERAL KNOWLEDGE | PLANNING

In this miniature crossword, the clues are listed randomly and are numbered for convenience only. It is up to you to figure out the placement of the 9 answers. To help you, we've inserted one letter in the grid, and this is the only occurrence of that letter in the completed puzzle.

CLUES

1. Faction
2. The Jets and the Sharks
3. Discounted
4. Angered expression
5. Determination
6. Air pollutant
7. Robin Cook thriller
8. Prophetic signs
9. Team beasts

How Many?

ANALYSIS | COMPUTATION

How many triangles of any size are in the figure below?

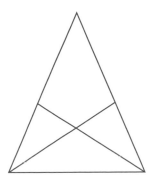

A. 3   B. 5   C. 8   D. 11

Answers on page 188.

Number Sequence

What is the next number in each of the sequences below?

1. 6, 16, 21, 31, 36, ___
   A. 51
   B. 41
   C. 46

2. 2, 12, 6, 16, 8, ___
   A. 18
   B. 4
   C. 16

3. 6, 18, 12, 36, 24, ___
   A. 48
   B. 72
   C. 16

4. 12, 24, 72, 144, 432, ___
   A. 576
   B. 1296
   C. 864

Visual Sequence

Which of the lettered figures continues the sequence?

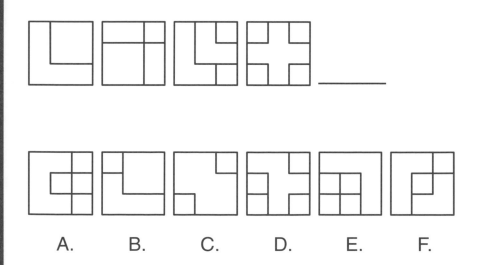

A.   B.   C.   D.   E.   F.

Answers on page 188.

Moon Base (Part I)

Study the lunar schematics before turning the page for a memory challenge.

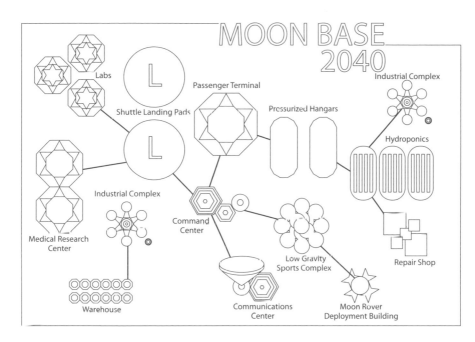

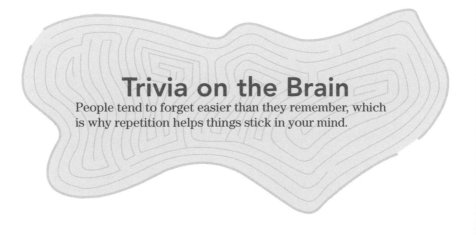

Trivia on the Brain

People tend to forget easier than they remember, which is why repetition helps things stick in your mind.

Moon Base (Part II)

MEMORY

(Do not read this until you have read the previous page!)

Now that you've studied the schematics, fill in the names of the buildings as they were labeled on page 153.

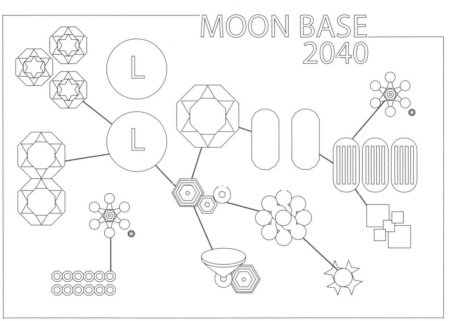

Trivia on the Brain

It's no accident that telephone numbers in the United States are 7 digits long. A human's short-term memory can process about 7 numbers at a time and store them just long enough to get to the phone and dial.

Answers on page 189.

Number Cross

Use each of the numbers listed below to complete this clue-less crossword grid. The puzzle has only one solution.

3 FIGURES

121

146

228

230

241

281

386

439

4 FIGURES

1452

1820

2124

2273

3502

4624

4641

4940

5 FIGURES

11381

14626

17382

17639

21590

26614

29680

30262

34492

41469

41613

42151

43682

46804

47871

49351

6 FIGURES

120241

145604

203665

205778

207681

235024

262924

324709

347340

351486

366796

386452

417293

446363

459337

Answer on page 189.

Quipu

ANALYSIS LOGIC

Which of the 3 Quipus (Incan devices for recording information) is identical to the one in the frame? Quipus are considered identical when they can be matched perfectly only by rotating pieces around the knots—they cannot be lifted or turned over. See the examples for further clarification.

EXAMPLE 1   **EXAMPLE 2**

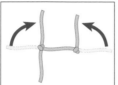 

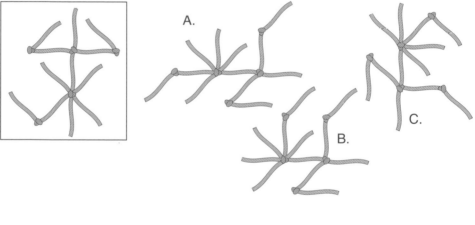

A.

B.

C.

Odd Word Out

ANALYSIS LOGIC

One of the words below doesn't fit in with the rest. The reason isn't based on parts of speech or the fact that one of them ends in a vowel. Can you find the odd one out?

scent, straight, numbing, graze, planter, dumbness

Answers on page 189.

Curve Fill

Fill in each heavy-outlined set of cells with the same number (0, 2, or 5) so that the sums given for each curved row and column and the 2 sections extending from the center oval are true. For further insight, see the example puzzle.

EXAMPLE

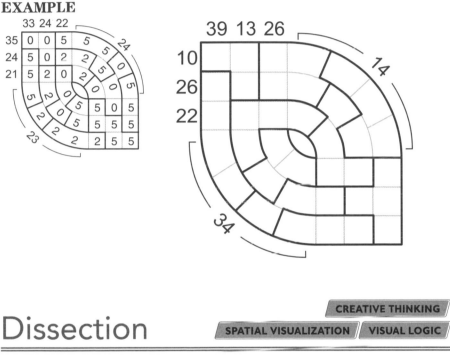

Dissection

Separate the figure into 2 identical parts following the grid lines. The parts may be rotated and/or mirrored.

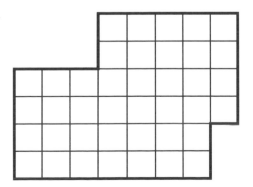

Answers on page 189.

Word Jigsaw

Fit the pieces into the frame to form common words reading across and down. There's no need to rotate the pieces; they'll fit as shown, with each piece used once.

LEVEL 4

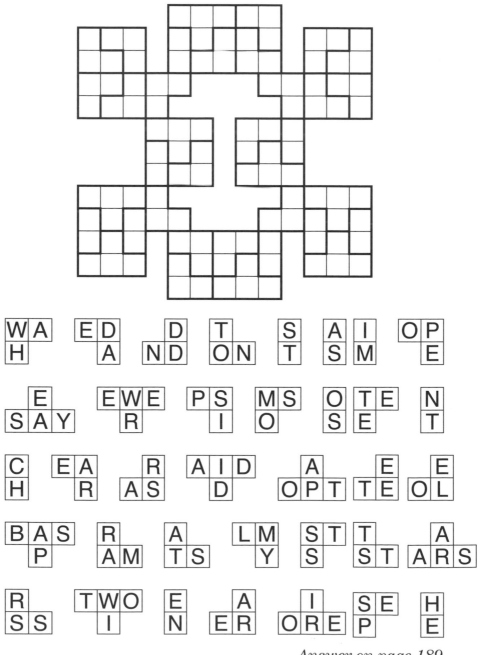

Answer on page 189.

Hitori

The object of this puzzle is to have a number appear only once in each row and column. By shading a number cell, you are effectively removing that number from its row and column. There's a catch though: Shaded number cells are never adjacent to one another in a row or column.

2	8	7	3	3	1	4	5	6
9	2	5	5	3	7	2	4	2
7	3	3	4	3	6	9	7	1
4	7	3	6	8	7	2	1	5
6	8	9	5	2	8	1	2	7
5	6	7	1	5	4	7	8	5
5	4	2	2	9	4	7	5	8
8	5	7	7	1	2	3	6	4
8	1	4	9	5	6	6	6	3

Cube Count

How many cubes are in the illustration below? Assume all rows and columns run to completion unless you actually see them end.

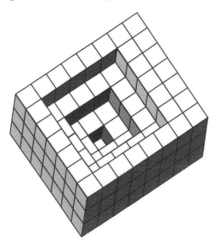

Hexagon Shade

ANALYSIS COMPUTATION

The figure below is a regular hexagon with a fraction of its area shaded. That shaded area is:

A. ⅔⁄₉   B. ¼   C. ⅓   D. ⁵⁄₁₂

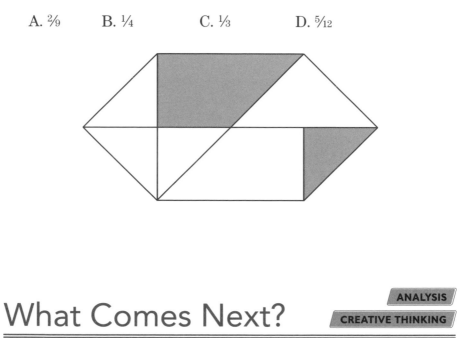

What Comes Next?

ANALYSIS

CREATIVE THINKING

Study the series of letters below. Every letter in each series is the first letter of a word, and all the words in each series are related. For example, if the first 4 letters of a series were M, V, E, M, they could stand for Mercury, Venus, Earth, and Mars. Logically, the next letter would be J, for Jupiter.

Continue each series below by discovering the next logical word.

1. P, C, S, L, C, M, ___

2. W, A, J, M, M, A, ___

3. O, B, C, B, R, C, ___

Answers on pages 189–190.

Some of These Words Are Misppelt (Part I)

Try to remember which captions are spelled wrong. Then turn the page for a memory challenge.

Gorilla

Salamandar

Pellican

Cubboard

Leprechaun

Harmonica

Doughnut

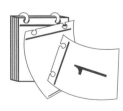

Calender

Dolfin

Some of These Words Are Misppelt (Part II)

MEMORY

(Do not read this until you have read the previous page!)

Which of these correctly spelled words were misspelled on page 161?

___ Dolphin

___ Doughnut

___ Leprechaun

___ Pelican

___ Calendar

___ Gorilla

___ Salamander

___ Cupboard

___ Harmonica

Fitting Words

GENERAL KNOWLEDGE   PLANNING

In this miniature crossword, the clues are listed randomly and are numbered for convenience only. It is up to you to figure out the placement of the 9 answers. To help you, we've inserted one letter in the grid, and this is the only occurrence of that letter in the completed puzzle.

CLUES

1. Double-reed woodwind

2. Soak, as a tea bag

3. Striplings

4. Footprint

5. Monastery head

6. Final notice?

7. Seems imminent

8. Statistical calculation

9. Part of LED

		M	

Answers on page 190.

Chain Grid Fill

To complete this puzzle, place the given words into the darkened chains in this grid. Words will run across, down, and diagonally along each darkened chain. It is up to you to figure out which letters go in the single white squares in the grid. When the grid is complete, each column of the grid will contain one of the following words: Arkansas, dragon, farmer, forces, future, military, prisoner, race cars, sounds, techno, tricycle. We filled in one word to get you started.

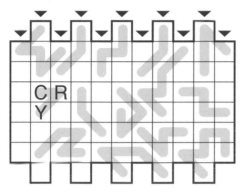

1. AIM, PRO, SON

2. CAME, DARK, RARE, RATE, TANG

3. FIRST, FLIRT, LENSE, SORRY

4. SEASON

Animal Count

$$\frac{4 \text{ Cows} + 2 \text{ Chickens}}{5 \text{ Ducks} + 3 \text{ Wolves}} = \frac{20}{?}$$

A. 11   B. 22   C. 44   D. 60

Answers on page 190.   163

Picture Rhyme

ATTENTION **VISUAL SEARCH**

There are 6 pairs of rhyming images in the illustration below. Can you find them all?

Trivia on the Brain

Memories triggered by scent form stronger, more intense emotional connections.

Answers on page 190.

Divided Triangle

If at least some segments of each side of a triangle pass through a square, what is the maximum number of distinct areas, not further subdivided, that could result?

A. 4   B. 7   C. 11   D. 17

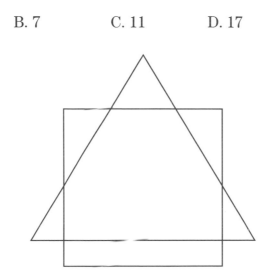

Visual Sequence

Which of the numbered figures completes the sequence?

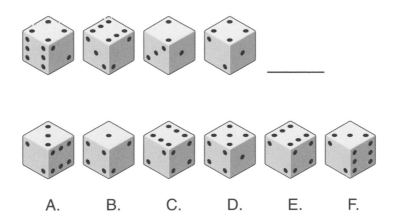

A.   B.   C.   D.   E.   F.

Answers on page 190.

Bird Photography

LOGIC

Gufferton Springs recently hired 5 wildlife photographers to capture some local birds on film for use in an upcoming tourism brochure. Each photographer was assigned a specific type of bird to photograph, and although they all went to Gufferton Springs Nature Preserve on the same morning, each photographer arrived there at a different time. Four of the 5 photographers were successful in capturing their assigned bird on film. Using only the following clues, match each photographer to the bird they were assigned, determine how many photos they were able to take during their excursion, and figure out what time they entered the nature preserve.

1. Kevin wasn't the last to enter the nature preserve, and he didn't come back with exactly 12 photographs.

2. The photographer who failed to snap any photos arrived at the preserve sometime before the one who photographed the vultures.

3. The woodpecker photographer (who wasn't Janice) arrived sometime before the one assigned to capture some osprey on film (who didn't return with exactly 12 photographs).

4. Of Kaitlyn and the photographer who was sent to capture pictures of a scarlet tanager, one came back with just 5 photographs, and the other was the third photographer to enter the preserve.

5. The 5 photographers were: the one who was sent to photograph a titmouse, the one who returned with the most photographs, Victor, and the last 2 to arrive at the preserve.

6. Of the photographer who arrived earliest at the nature preserve and the one who snapped the most photographs, one went looking for vultures and the other for scarlet tanagers.

Time	Birdwatcher	Photographs	Bird
6:30 A.M.			
7:00 A.M.			
8:15 A.M.			
8:45 A.M.			
9:30 A.M.			

L
E
V
E
L

4

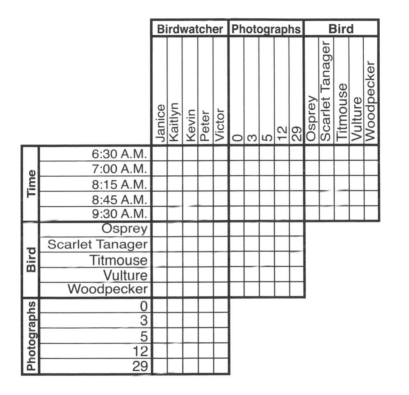

Cousins

ANALYSIS COMPUTATION

I have 3 cousins. If you multiply their ages, you get 36. I have a 1 in 8 chance of getting all 3 ages correct on the first try. If I eliminate the possibility of any of the cousins being 1 year old, what is my probability of getting the ages correct?

A. 1 in 2   B. 1 in 3   C. 1 in 4   D. 1 in 6

L
E
V
E
L

4

Cube Fold

Below is an unfolded cube. Only 3 of the cubes below (marked A–E) can possibly represent this cube when folded. Which 3?

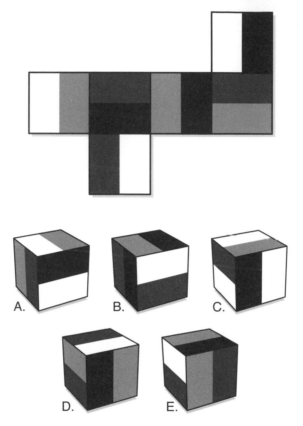

A. B. C.

D. E.

Trivia on the Brain

Some foods that contain choline—such as soy, peanuts, and eggs—may improve alertness and memory while relieving stress and fatigue. Choline builds the neuro-transmitters that pass electrical impulses between brain cells.

Answers on page 190.

Remember Me—
If You Can (Part I)

The illustrations below may or may not have the right captions. Study these items for a minute, then turn the page for a memory challenge.

Lawnmower

Vise

Gargoyle

Golf club

Hurricane lamp

Palm tree

Remember Me— If You Can (Part II)

MEMORY

(Do not read this until you have read the previous page!)

Check off items you saw pictured on page 169, regardless of the captions.

___ Gravy boat

___ Alligator

___ Hurricane lamp

___ Camera

___ Fire hydrant

___ Jigsaw puzzle

___ Vise

___ Golf club

Fitting Words

GENERAL KNOWLEDGE **PLANNING**

In this miniature crossword, the clues are listed randomly and are numbered for convenience only. It is up to you to figure out the placement of the 9 answers. To help you out, we've inserted one letter in the grid, and this is the only occurrence of that letter in the completed puzzle.

CLUES

1. Not to mention
2. Destiny
3. Wise guys?
4. Peer
5. Pipsqueak
6. They contain bronchioles
7. Pastel hue
8. Summertime restaurant adjunct
9. Sushi wrap

Answers on page 190.

Answers

Party Time (page 6)

1. Number on top left balloon; 2. skull and crossbones missing on boy's hat; 3. candle missing on cake; 4. clown's nose is colored; 5. second balloon from left is missing tie; 6. robot's antenna is different shape; 7. robot's ice cream is not dripping; 8. robot is missing dial; 9. clock time is different; 10. tiger is missing a stripe.

Number Cross (page 7)

Word Jigsaw (page 8)

```
N O R
I N A N E
P E N A L
    G Y M
```

Add-a-Word (page 8)

1. soda; 2. water; 3. beer; 4. tea; 5. wine; 6. milk

Take a Load Off! (Parts I & II) (pages 9–10)

Stool, folding chair, armchair, rocking chair, office chair, director's chair

Number Sequence

(page 10)
C. 441. The sum of each set of 3 digits is 9.

Monsters (page 11)

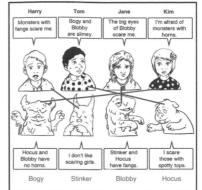

Cube Fold (page 12)

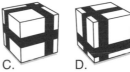

C.   D.

Grid Fill (page 13)

```
F I S T S
B R A U N
D R E A M
S O N I C
P A T I O
S T R I P
```

Addagram (page 13)

The missing letter is **A**.
Martini, margarita, Bloody Mary, tequila sunrise

Number Sequence

(page 14)
1. A. 20 (+2, +3, +4, +5, +6)
2. C. 16 (+2, +4, +2, +4, +2)
3. C. 26 (+3, +4, +5, +6, +7)
4. C. 10 (+4, −2, +4, −2, +4)

Visual Sequence (page 15)

A. Each subsequent animal has 2 additional legs.

Pyramid (page 15)

The number in each brick is the sum of the 2 bricks below it.

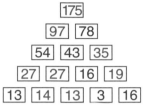

```
          175
        97   78
      54   43   35
    27   27   16   19
  13   14   13   3   16
```

Odd One Out (page 16)

F. The other figures have the square placed on the tip of a backward **L**.

Addagram (page 16)

The missing letter is **U**.
Iguana, granule, meringue, greyhound

Convention of Action Figures (Parts I & II)

(pages 17–18)
1. Any 3 of these 7: Acrobat, Roller Skater, Martial Artist, Rodeo Cowboy, Weight Lifter, Archer, Baseball Player;
2. Wyoming; 3. 2

Grid Fill (page 18)

```
C I G A R
S T O R K
T R E E S
B O A S T
A N G R Y
T A B L E
```

Add-a-Word (page 19)

1. book; 2. story; 3. tale; 4. play;
5. letter; 6. note

Word Jigsaw (page 19)

```
E G G
M A L E S
U S U R P
  E R A
```

Collection of Cs (page 20)

1. camera; 2. can; 3. candy;
4. cane; 5. cap; 6. car; 7. cheese;
8. chicken; 9. clouds;
10. computer; 11. cowboy boots;
12. cows; 13. cubes; 14. cup

Analogies (page 21)

1. B. short; 2. C. drink;
3. A. play; 4. B. succeed

Number Sequence

(page 21)
7. $2+1=3$; $1+3=4$; $3+4=7$

Number Cross (page 22)

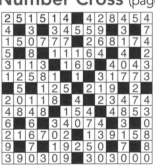

```
2 5 1 5 1 4   4 2 8 4 5 4
4   3   3 4 5 5 9   3   7
1 5 0 7 7 7   2 6 8 1 7 4
5   8   1 1 1 6 4   4   2
3 1 1 3   1 6 9   4 0 4 3
1 2 5 8 1   1   3 1 7 7 3
  5   1 2 5   2 1 9   2
2 0 1 1 8   4   2 3 4 7 4
4 8 4 8   1 5 4   4 8 5 3
6 6   6 3 4 0 7 4   3   0
2 1 6 7 0 2   1 3 9 1 5 8
9   7   1 9 2 5 0   7   8
3 9 0 3 0 9   3 0 3 0 0 0
```

Pattern Placement

(page 23)

Teddy Bears (page 24)

Grid Fill (page 25)

```
S T O R M
D R O N E
A C O R N
S K A T E
S A L A D
U L T R A
```

Dissection (page 25)

What to Wear? (page 26)

Mind Stretcher (page 27)

D. In row 1, the times read 1, 3, 5, and 7. In row 2, the times read 2, 4, 6, and 8. In row 3, the times should read 3, 6, 9, and 12.

Analogies (page 28)

1. C. map; 2. A. lick; 3. B. hungry; 4. C. cut

Game Board (Parts I & II) (pages 29–30)

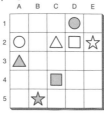

Max-Die-Sum (pages 30)

The maximum possible sum is 15 (4+5+6).

Number Cross (page 31)

Broken Heart (page 32)

No. There are an odd number of boxes (27), making an even split impossible.

Mystery List (page 32)

Billy's typing was off by one key to the right. What he wants is a: dog, bike, skateboard, toy robot, iPod.

Beastly Metaphors (Parts I & II) (pages 33–34)

1. B; 2. D; 3. C; 4. C

Number Sequence
(page 34)
D. 82. The sequence is +7, +9, +11, +13, +15, +17.

Add-a-Word (page 35)
1. duck; 2. goose; 3. swan;
4. dove; 5. pigeon; 6. eagle

Word Jigsaw (page 35)

	S	A	Y	
A	L	O	N	E
G	I	F	T	S
O	P	T		

Cube Count (page 36)
15

It's a Big Block (page 36)
There are 11 houses in the row.

Analogies (page 37)
1. A. construct; 2. C. think;
3. A. search; 4. B. sing

Quilt Quest (page 38)

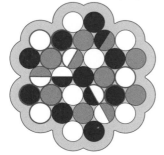

Odd One Out (page 39)
D. The other figures are replicated within their intersections.

After the Rain (page 39)
There is no chance. Five hours later is 1:00 A.M., and even if a night rainbow were to occur, it would have dim colors that our eyes would perceive in grayscale.

Fitting Words (page 40)

T	A	B	O	O
E	R	R	O	R
S	E	I	Z	E
T	A	M	E	S

Quipu (page 41)
B

Word Jigsaw (page 42)

		L	O	G
C	R	E	D	O
O	U	T	D	O
Y	E	S		

Deal Me In (page 42)
S. C(lubs), D(iamonds), H(earts), S(pades)

Moon Base (Parts I & II)
(pages 43–44)

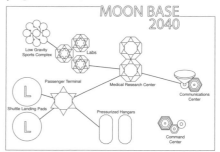

Squared Cubes Squared
(pages 44)
They are equal. A dozen dozen is 144. Square that and you get 20,736. Cubed, that is 8,916,100,448,256. A dozen dozen cubed is 2,985,984. If you square that, the result is the same—8,916,100,448,256.

What Comes Next?
(page 45)
C. The arrow turns 90 degrees clockwise from one shape to another.

Letter Logic (pages 46–47)

Sleepless in Seattle
(page 47)
1. Bottom of birdcage is missing; 2. windowpanes are different; 3. picture is upside down; 4. bookcase sitting on bedpost; 5. man has 2 different pajama sleeves; 6. man's body disappears in pillow; 7. part of lamp base missing; 8. rug pattern changes; 9. footstool leg is missing; 10. cat coming out of footboard

Missing Number (page 48)
6. The number in the middle of each figure is ¼ the sum of the 4 numbers surrounding it.

Dissection (page 48)

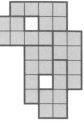

How Many? (page 49)
There are 12 triangles in all.

Grid Fill (page 49)

```
B E A S T
C R A M S
H A P P Y
C H O I R
I C I N G
D R A P E
```

Visual Sequence (page 50)
D. Outlines of the 4 suits of cards are halved.

Fitting Words (page 50)

```
N A K E D
A L I V E
P I L E S
S T O R K
```

Number Cross (page 51)

Cube Fold (page 52)

A.   E.

Area Code (page 53)

They have the same area. (Radius is equal to ½ diameter, making a circle with a radius of 2 equal to one with a diameter of 4.)

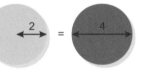

Hearty Greetings (Parts I & II) (pages 53–54)

Love, chocolate, honey, sweetie, lamb, pet

Word Jigsaw (page 54)

Curve Fill (page 55)

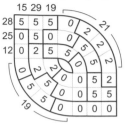

Add-a-Word (page 55)

1. piano; 2. drum; 3. horn; 4. whistle; 5. gun

Cat Finder (page 56)

Number Sequence (page 56)

3. $15-9=6$; $9-6=3$; $6-3=3$

Dot Movement (page 57)

B

Analogies (page 58)

1. B. wet; 2. A. pound; 3. C. amusement; 4. B. iron

Cast-a-Word (page 58)

1. A B D F T Y
2. C H I O V W
3. E G K M P U
4. L N Q R S X

Pattern Placement
(page 59)

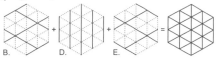

Dart Toss (page 60)
B. 12. The 4 numbers that total 100 are 15, 18, 23, and 44.

Round Trip
(Parts I & II) (pages 61–62)
Tomato, disco ball, button, globe, target in crosshairs, yin and yang symbol

Fitting Words (page 62)

Odd One Out (page 63)
C. It is the only concave figure. If you can draw a line between 2 points inside a figure and have that line also pass outside the figure, it is concave.

Quipu (page 63)
C

Cube Fold (page 64)

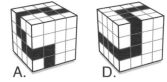

Bottled Up (page 65)

← A.

Role Models (Parts I & II)
(pages 65–66)
1. *Robinson Crusoe*;
2. Honolulu; 3. *The Thin Man*;
4. Charlie Chan; 5. four years

Word Jigsaw (page 66)

Analogies (page 67)
1. B. leg; 2. C. dangerous;
3. A. perish; 4. B. sprinkle

Perfect Circle (page 67)
No. These 2 pieces will form an oval, not a perfect circle.

Add-a-Word (page 68)
1. driver; 2. club; 3. green;
4. trap; 5. ball; 6. wolf

Matching Sticks (page 68)

Place Settings (page 69)

D. 36. Half of 46 is 23, making everyone 23 numbers apart from one another.

Game Board (Parts I & II) (pages 69–70)

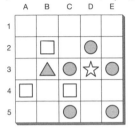

What Comes Next?

(page 70)

1. R. Books of the Bible: G(enesis), E(xodus), L(eviticus), N(umbers), D(euteronomy), J(oshua), J(udges), R(uth);
2. R. Baseball scoring positions: P(itcher), C(atcher), F(irst baseman), S(econd baseman), T(hird baseman), S(hortstop), L(eft fielder), C(enter fielder), R(ight fielder); 3. B. Billiard balls: Y(ellow), B(lue), R(ed), P(urple), O(range), G(reen), B(rown), B(lack)

Square Search (page 71)

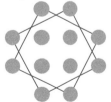

Square Donut (page 72)

There are 42 square outlines of 3 different sizes.

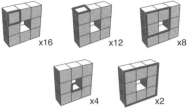

Analogies (page 72)

1. B. precinct; 2. C. class;
3. A. cheese

Pythagorize It! (page 73)

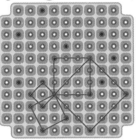

Letter Logic (pages 74–75)

How Many? (page 75)
D. 27. There are 16 one-cell triangles, 7 four-cell triangles, 3 nine-cell triangles, and 1 sixteen-cell triangle.

Grid Fill (page 76)

F	R	A	M	E	
A	G	A	I	N	
D	R	A	F	T	
E	N	T	E	R	
B	E	R	R	Y	
B	L	I	M	P	

Longest Snake (page 76)

Number Sequence
(page 77)
1. A. 24 (+3, +6, +3, +6, +3)
2. B. 21 (+5, +4, +3, +2, +1)
3. A. 31 (+2, +4, +6, +8, +10)
4. C. 167 (+11, +22, +33, +44, +55)

Odd One Out (page 78)
A. The other shapes have an equal ratio of light to dark boxes.

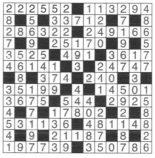
A.

Quilt Quest (page 78)
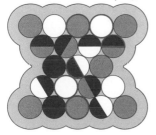

Analogies (page 79)
1. C. leaf; 2. A. snowflake; 3. A. subject; 4. C. fish

Days of the Week (page 79)
B. 2

Visual Sequence (page 80)
E. Each clock shows the time 8 hours and 7 minutes ahead of the previous one.

Marathon (page 80)
B. 45

Number Cross (page 81)

2	2	2	5	5	2		1	1	3	2	9	4
8		5		3	3	7	1	2		7		8
2	8	6	3	2	2		2	4	9	1	6	6
7		9		2	5	1	7	0		9		5
3	5	2	5		4	9	1		3	6	1	7
4	6	1	4	1		3		2	4	7	4	7
	8		3	7	4		2	1	0		3	
3	5	1	9	9		4		1	4	5	0	1
3	6	7	5		5	4	4		2	9	2	5
4		7		1	7	8	0	2		2		8
5	3	1	1	3	6		4	8	1	1	4	8
4		9		2	1	1	8	7		8		2
1	9	7	7	3	9		3	5	0	7	8	6

Koi Pond (page 82)
1. pad turned to flower; 2. tail smaller; 3. pad rotated; 4. cut in pad widened; 5. flower missing petal; 6. fin raised on fish's body; 7. fin missing; 8. black koi's fin shorter; 9. pad gone; 10. white koi has whisker; 11. black koi's scales changed direction; 12. pad added beneath flower; 13. petal missing on water lily; 14. water lily smaller; 15. flower added

Quipu (page 83)

C

Cube Paint (page 84)

You would need 14 gallons of paint. There are 42 external sides (the same number as the number of faces on 7 cubes). Because 2 gallons are needed to paint 1 cube, you would need 2×7 or 14 gallons of paint to cover the figure.

Cast-a-Word (page 84)

1. A B I J M S
2. C E G N P W
3. D F H K O Y
4. L R T U V Z

Number Sequence

(page 85)

1. C. 36 (+7, +6, +7, +6, +7)
2. A. 90 (×2, +5, ×2, +5, ×2)
3. C. 38 (+14, −7, +14, −7, +14)
4. B. 4 (+1, ×½, +1, ×½, +1)

Missing Figure (page 86)

C. It is the only grid left to complete all 3 symbols being positioned in each of the 9 boxes in the 3×3 grid.

Matchmaker (page 87)

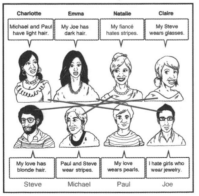

Some Change? (page 87)

7. Three dimes, a nickel, and 3 pennies.

Word Jigsaw (page 88)

Visual Sequence (page 89)

D. If 2 or more neighboring circles have the same color, they all change color, cyclically.

Chain Grid Fill (page 89)

Detective Work! (page 90)

Name That Icon (Parts I & II) (pages 91–92)

Christ over Rio de Janeiro, Pyramids of Egypt, Sphinx at Giza, Leaning Tower of Pisa, Great Wall of China, Eiffel Tower, Sydney Opera House

Area Code (page 92)

All the letters have the same area of 6 square units.

Visualize This! (page 93)

Blue sock, jacket, belt, pants, red sock, tie, right gym shoe, cowboy hat, white shirt, left gym shoe, winter coat, boxer shorts, waistcoat

Cast-a-Word (page 93)

1. A C H M N Y
2. B D I P V Z
3. E F S T U X
4. K L O Q R W

Cube Fold (page 94)

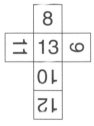

Odd Word Out (page 94)

RIGHT. The other words sound like one of the 5 human senses.

Fitting Words (page 95)

O	P	I	U	M
D	O	D	G	E
D	U	E	L	S
S	T	A	Y	S

Addagram (page 95)

The missing letter is **M.** Hermit, emerald, admiral, ignoramus

Number Cross (page 96)

Analogies (page 97)

1. A. DVD; 2. C. complex;
3. A. criminal; 4. C. cow

Meeting Point (page 97)

A meeting point is always reached simultaneously.

Paper Cut (page 98)

C

Add-a-Word (page 98)

1. potato; 2. pepper; 3. banana;
4. bean; 5. onion; 6. rice

Quipu (page 99)

A

Arrows (Parts I & II)

(pages 99–100)

←	↑
↑	↓

What Comes Next?

(page 100)

1. F. Musical staff lines: E(very) G(ood) B(oy) D(oes) F(ine);
2. S. Great Lakes: H(uron), O(ntario), M(ichigan), E(rie), S(uperior); 3. D. Money: P(enny), N(ickel), D(ime), Q(uarter), H(alf-dollar) D(ollar)

Quilt Quest (page 101)

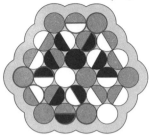

Odd Word Out (page 101)

Cupboard. The other words contain the letters A, B, C, D, and E. Cupboard has only A, B, C, and D.

Brothers and Sisters
(page 102)

Word Spiral (page 102)

Lawnmowers

From 0 to 100 (page 103)

0. It appears 12 times.

Visual Sequence (page 103)

B. A side is added to both the interior and exterior shapes with each progression.

Knot Problem (page 104)

Either A or B

Cast-a-Word (page 104)

1. A F J N P W
2. B G O S Y Z
3. C D H I R T
4. E K L U V X

Pattern Placement
(page 105)

Cube Fold (page 106)

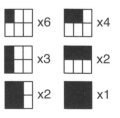

What Type? (page 106)

B. 10. Each typist finishes one page in 5 minutes, so 2 pages can be completed in 10 minutes. Since we need 20 pages, we need 10 typists.

Not Exactly! (Parts I & II)
(pages 107–108)

1. the Andes; 2. marsupials; 3. a nerve; 4. orange; 5. gypsum

Fitting Words (page 108)

R	A	Z	O	R
A	L	O	N	E
M	I	N	C	E
S	T	E	E	L

How Many? (page 109)

18

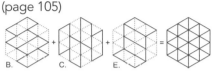

Add-a-Word (page 109)

1. glove; 2. field; 3. base; 4. bat; 5. ball; 6. team

Letter Logic (pages 110–111)

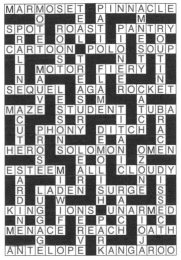

A Passion for Fashion (Parts I & II) (pages 111–112)

Tank top, overalls, bell-bottoms, platform shoes, turtleneck sweater, cargo pants

Dissection (page 112)

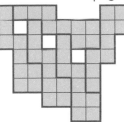

Curve Fill (page 113)

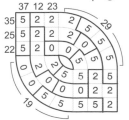

Number Sequence
(page 113)

C. $\frac{1}{15}$. There are 2 sequences here. Starting with the first fraction and looking at every other one, you have: $\frac{1}{5}$, $\frac{1}{7}$, $\frac{1}{9}$, $\frac{1}{11}$, and $\frac{1}{13}$. Starting with the other set, you have $\frac{1}{3}$, $\frac{1}{5}$, $\frac{1}{7}$, $\frac{1}{9}$, and $\frac{1}{11}$. So, $\frac{1}{15}$ completes the first sequence.

Word Jigsaw (page 114)

Cube Count (page 115)

125 cubes are completely hidden.

Number Sequence
(page 116)

1. B. 36 ($\times 2$, $\times \frac{3}{4}$, $\times 2$, $\times \frac{3}{4}$, $\times 2$)
2. A. 125 ($\times 5$, $\times \frac{1}{2}$, $\times 5$, $\times \frac{1}{2}$, $\times 5$)
3. C. 38 ($1+7=8$; $7+8=15$; $8+15=23$; $15+23=38$)
4. B. 52 ($12+1=13$; $12+13=25$; $25+1=26$; $25+26=51$; $51+1=52$)

How to Survive an Arctic Night (Parts I & II)
(pages 117–118)

1. Twenty to 60 degrees Fahrenheit; 2. snow knife; 3. machete (or sword); 4. for ventilation; 5. body heat

Hidden Word (page 118)

Nearsightedness

Number Cross (page 119)

1	6	3	5	1	3	■	2	3	5	2	4	2
5	■	3	■	3	3	0	2	4	■	1	■	2
1	1	5	3	1	6	■	1	2	2	4	0	4
2	■	3	■	3	3	1	3	4	■	0	■	0
3	1	3	2	■	2	4	0	■	2	6	2	6
1	3	2	1	2	■	3	■	3	4	4	4	5
■	1	■	2	6	1	■	2	5	2	■	4	■
1	2	2	2	5	■	3	■	1	0	1	6	2
3	1	4	6	■	1	3	1	■	1	6	6	5
5	■	0	■	3	0	5	2	2	■	5	■	3
1	1	1	5	6	2	■	2	2	0	6	0	0
1	■	0	■	1	6	6	6	6	■	5	■	5
3	3	5	4	0	3	■	3	5	6	6	6	6

Cube Fold (page 120)

Quilt Quest (page 120)

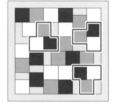

Character Substitute
(page 121)

When typed out without the SHIFT key pressed, these characters are odd numbers 1 through 7. The missing one is 9 or "(" with the SHIFT key pressed.

! # % & (

1 3 5 7 9

Quipu (page 121)

B

Analogies (page 122)

1. C. rooster; 2. A. delighted;
3. A. tsunami; 4. B. red

Pythagorize It! (page 123)

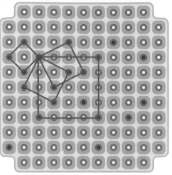

Cube Fold (page 124)

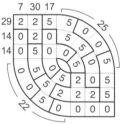

D.   E.

Anagram (page 124)

C. A country. Unscrambled, the letters spell Argentina, so the answer is C.

Curve Fill (page 125)

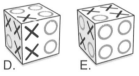

Add-a-Word (page 125)

1. road; 2. street; 3. path; 4. alley;
5. crescent; 6. trail

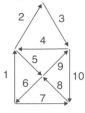

Figure Trace (page 126)

Letter-In (page 126)

B. These 3 rows are fragments of a keyboard.

Pattern Recognition

(page 127)

D. Multiply the top 2 numbers in each figure and add the number on the bottom left to arrive at the number on the bottom right.

A Musical Discovery

(pages 128–129)

Year	Title	Instrument	Key
1863	Eliza	Violin	C minor
1864	Beatrice	Clarinet	D minor
1865	Heloise	Piano	A minor
1866	Margot	Cello	E minor
1867	Theresa	Flute	C major

Hitori (page 129)

Animal Phrasing (page 130)

1. Tree frog; 2. barn owl; 3. box turtle; 4. jackrabbit; 5. earthworm; 6. fruit fly; 7. pack rat.

Triangular Sums (page 131)

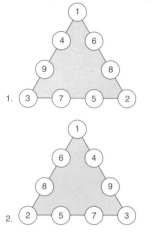

Add-a-Word (page 131)

1. fiddle; 2. bomb; 3. bullet; 4. arrow; 5. rifle; 6. sword

Overlapping Sheets

(page 132)

5 sheets

Visualize This! (page 132)

Ditch, crossroads, hill, signpost, bridge, aqueduct, fence, wishing well, scarecrow, restaurant, canal lock, traffic lights

Word Jigsaw (page 133)

Odd One Out (page 134)

Figure B. Figure C is the same as Figure A rotated 180 degrees. Figure E is the same as Figure D flipped along its horizontal axis.

Game Time (page 134)

D. Win by 29. Minnesota beat Baylor by 32, and Oklahoma beat Baylor by 3. If Minnesota were to play Oklahoma, they would win 32−3, or by 29 points.

Visual Sequence (page 135)

F. Moving clockwise from the top-left corner, matches meeting at a corner are flipped over. Middle matches turn 90 degrees clockwise with each move.

Mini-Cross (Part I)

(page 135)

M	A	C	A	W
A	W	A	R	E
C	O	N	N	S
S	L	E	E	T

Mini-Cross (Part II)

(page 136)
Aware, west, AWOL, cane, macaw, Macs

Cast-a-Word (page 136)

1. A H Q R W Y
2. B E J N T U
3. C G I L P V
4. D F K O S Z

Chain Grid Fill (page 137)

Addagram (page 137)

The missing letter is **R.** Turnip, archer, barnacle, pertinent

Cube Fold (page 138)

B.   E.

Fitting Words (page 138)

Q	U	A	R	T
U	N	D	U	E
A	D	D	L	E
D	O	S	E	S

Knot Problem (page 139)

B is linked.

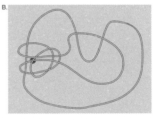

Triangular Pattern

(page 140)
The missing letter is **R.** Starting with the **W** at the top of the first triangle, the letters spell "What's your answeR?"

Quilt Quest (page 140)

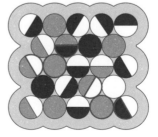

Which Dog Is Mine?
(page 141)

Pop Quiz (page 141)
E. Anteater. The other 4 are marsupials, characterized by a pouch in which females carry their young.

Number Cross (page 142)

Odd One Out (page 143)
D. The other shapes take up 8 square units each; D takes up 7.5 square units.

Quipu (page 143)
B and C

Missing Number (page 144)
The number 1. Add the top and bottom number in each diamond and divide that by the sum of the 2 side numbers.

What Comes Next?
(page 145)
1. R. Birthstones: G(arnet), A(methyst), A(quamarine), D(iamond), E(merald), A(lexandrite), R(uby);
2. V. Rainbow colors: R(ed), O(range), Y(ellow), G(reen), B(lue), I(ndigo), V(iolet);
3. S. Ordinal numbers: F(irst), S(econd), T(hird), F(ourth), F(ifth), S(ixth), S(eventh)

Game Board (Parts I & II)
(pages 145–146)

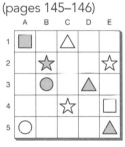

Chain Grid Fill (page 146)

K	C	B	P	B
C	L	S	O	P	U	S	A	B	A	Y
H	O	T	M	O	D	T	S	U	N	O
A	N	O	P	T	D	E	S	R	K	D
R	D	G	O	A	H	A	O	E	R	E
G	I	I	S	T	I	M	V	A	U	L
E	K	E	E	O	S	Y	E	U	P	S
	E		D		T		R		T	

Missing Figure (page 147)

C. In each pair, (1, 2; 3, 4), the second exterior shape is the same as the first shape's interior.

1.   2.   3.   4.

Dissection (page 147)

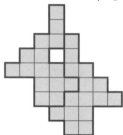

Knot Problem (page 148)

B

Cube Fold (page 149)

C.   E.

One of These Things...

(page 149)

E. 38524. Its digits total 22 while the others total 20.

Pattern Placement

(page 150)

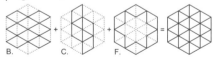

B.   +   C.   +   F.   =

Grid Fill (page 150)

Fitting Words (page 151)

S	C	O	W	L
M	O	X	I	E
O	M	E	N	S
G	A	N	G	S

How Many? (page 151)

C. 8

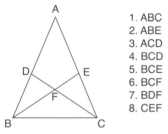

1. ABC
2. ABE
3. ACD
4. BCD
5. BCE
6. BCF
7. BDF
8. CEF

Number Sequence

(page 152)

1. C. 46 (+10, +5, +10, +5, +10)
2. A. 18 (+10, ×½, +10, ×½, +10)
3. B. 72 (×3, ×⅔, ×3, ×⅔, ×3)
4. C. 864 (×2, ×3, ×2, ×3, ×2)

Visual Sequence (page 152)

E. Each subsequent figure has one additional square.

Moon Base (Parts I & II)
(pages 153–154)

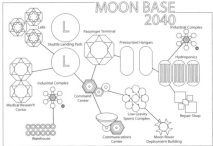

Number Cross (page 155)

Quipu (page 156)
B

Odd Word Out (page 156)
Planter. It is the only word that does not have a silent letter.

Curve Fill (page 157)

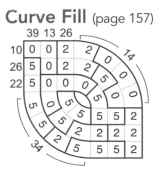

Dissection (page 157)

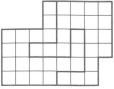

Word Jigsaw (page 158)

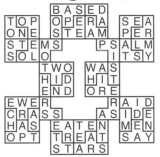

Hitori (page 159)

Cube Count (page 159)
There are 133 cubes in the illustration.

Hexagon Shade (page 160)
C. ⅓

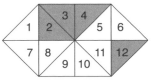

What Comes Next?
(page 160)
1. C. Army rankings: P(rivate), C(orporal), S(ergeant), L(ieutenant), C(aptain), M(ajor), C(olonel); 2. J. The first 7 presidents: W(ashington), A(dams), J(efferson), M(adison), M(onroe), A(dams), J(ackson); 3. F. The most recent presidents in reverse order: O(bama), B(ush), C(linton), B(ush), R(eagan), C(arter), F(ord)

Some of These Words Are Misppelt (Parts I & II)
(pages 161–162)
Dolphin, calendar, salamander, pelican, cupboard

Fitting Words (page 162)

L	O	O	M	S
A	B	B	O	T
D	I	O	D	E
S	T	E	E	P

Chain Grid Fill (page 163)

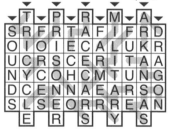

Animal Count (page 163)
B. 22. Four cows and 2 chickens have 20 legs; 5 ducks and 3 wolves have 22 legs.

Picture Rhyme (page 164)
1. Nun/sun; 2. batter/hatter; 3. coach/roach; 4. rower/mower; 5. miner/liner; 6. cook/book

Divided Triangle (page 165)
B. 7

Visual Sequence (page 165)
C. The die is rolled along the ground axis north, then west, then south, then east.

Bird Photography
(pages 166–167)

Time	Birdwatcher	Photographs	Bird
6:30 A.M.	Victor	5	Scarlet Tanager
7:00 A.M.	Kevin	0	Titmouse
8:15 A.M.	Kaitlyn	29	Vulture
8:45 A.M.	Peter	12	Woodpecker
9:30 A.M.	Janice	3	Osprey

Cousins (page 167)
B. 1 in 3. Eliminating one age narrows the range of guesses. Without the 1, you only have 3 options: 2, 3, and 6; 2, 2, and 9; or 3, 3, and 4.

Cube Fold (page 168)

B. D. E.

Remember Me—If You Can (Parts I & II)
(pages 169–170)
Alligator, camera, jigsaw puzzle, vise

Fitting Words (page 170)

K	A	R	M	A
E	Q	U	A	L
L	U	N	G	S
P	A	T	I	O

Index